# DU UND ICH 2

## A

For each exercise you are given instructions about how you and your partner should work together. You are also given an example of the sort of dialogue the exercise requires. This is to help you — it is not the answer to any of the questions.

| Contents | | Page | Contents | | Page |
|---|---|---|---|---|---|
| **Section 1** | **Personal identification** | | Exercise 4 | Taking down a shopping list | 17 |
| Exercise 1 | Identify the picture | 3 | Exercise 5 | Shopping — how much to buy | 18 |
| Exercise 2 | Check the information | 4 | Exercise 6 | Meals for the weekend | 19 |
| Exercise 3 | Describe the face | 5 | | | |
| Exercise 4 | Draw the face | 6 | | | |
| Exercise 5 | What are you taking on holiday? | 7 | **Section 4** | **Shops and shopping** | |
| Exercise 6 | Packing | 8 | Exercise 1 | The shops | 20 |
| Exercise 7 | Phoning ahead | 9 | Exercise 2 | Where are they going and why? | 21 |
| Exercise 8 | Check the facts | 10 | Exercise 3 | At the shops | 22 |
| | | | Exercise 4 | At the post office | 23 |
| **Section 2** | **Location** | | | | |
| Exercise 1 | Where does she live? | 11 | | | |
| Exercise 2 | Where does he live? | 12 | **Section 5** | **Travel by bus and tram** | |
| Exercise 3 | Where do you live? | 13 | Exercise 1 | Destinations | 24 |
| | | | Exercise 2 | Which bus or tram route? | 25 |
| **Section 3** | | | Exercise 3 | Where is the bus stop you want? | 26 |
| **Food and quantities** | | | Exercise 4 | Which bus is it and where is the stop? | 27 |
| Exercise 1 | Test your partner | 14 | Exercise 5 | How do I get there and where do I get off? | 28 |
| Exercise 2 | Good and bad ideas for a picnic | 15 | | | |
| Exercise 3 | Quantities | 16 | | | |

(cont.)

# DU UND ICH 2

| Contents | | Page | Contents | | Page |
|---|---|---|---|---|---|
| **Section 6** | **Travel by train** | | Exercise 2 | Booking in | 39 |
| Exercise 1 | Train times and platforms | 29 | Exercise 3 | Campsite amenities | 40 |
| Exercise 2 | When does it leave and when does it arrive? | 30 | Exercise 4 | At the campsite | 41 |
| Exercise 3 | Train times, platforms and tickets | 31 | Exercise 5 | Checking the details | 42 |
| Exercise 4 | Timetables | 32 | **Section 9** | **Holiday activities** | |
| | | | Exercise 1 | Holiday activities | 43 |
| **Section 7** | **The youth hostel** | | Exercise 2 | What can you do and what does it cost? | 44 |
| Exercise 1 | Rooms in the youth hostel | 33 | Exercise 3 | Which holiday centre suits them? A puzzle | 45 |
| Exercise 2 | Where the rooms are | 34 | | | |
| Exercise 3 | Where are the dormitories? | 35 | | | |
| Exercise 4 | Making a simple booking | 36 | | | |
| Exercise 5 | Making a more complicated booking | 37 | **Section 10** | **Holiday plans** | |
| | | | Exercise 1 | Where are they going and when? | 46 |
| **Section 8** | **Camping** | | Exercise 2 | Check the facts | 47 |
| Exercise 1 | What do you say when you book in? | 38 | Exercise 3 | Where are you going on holiday? | 48 |

# 1 PERSONAL IDENTIFICATION

### Exercise 1  Identify the picture

In this exercise you and your partner take it in turns to read out the description of a person to each other. Your partner identifies the person that you describe by giving the appropriate letter. Your partner will tell you if you have got it right.

Zum Beispiel:  
**A** Sie hat lange Haare.  
Sie hat eine Brille an.  
Sie hat eine lange Nase.  
Sie hat blaue Augen.  
**B** Ist das/es K?  
**A** Ja. Richtig. Du bist dran.

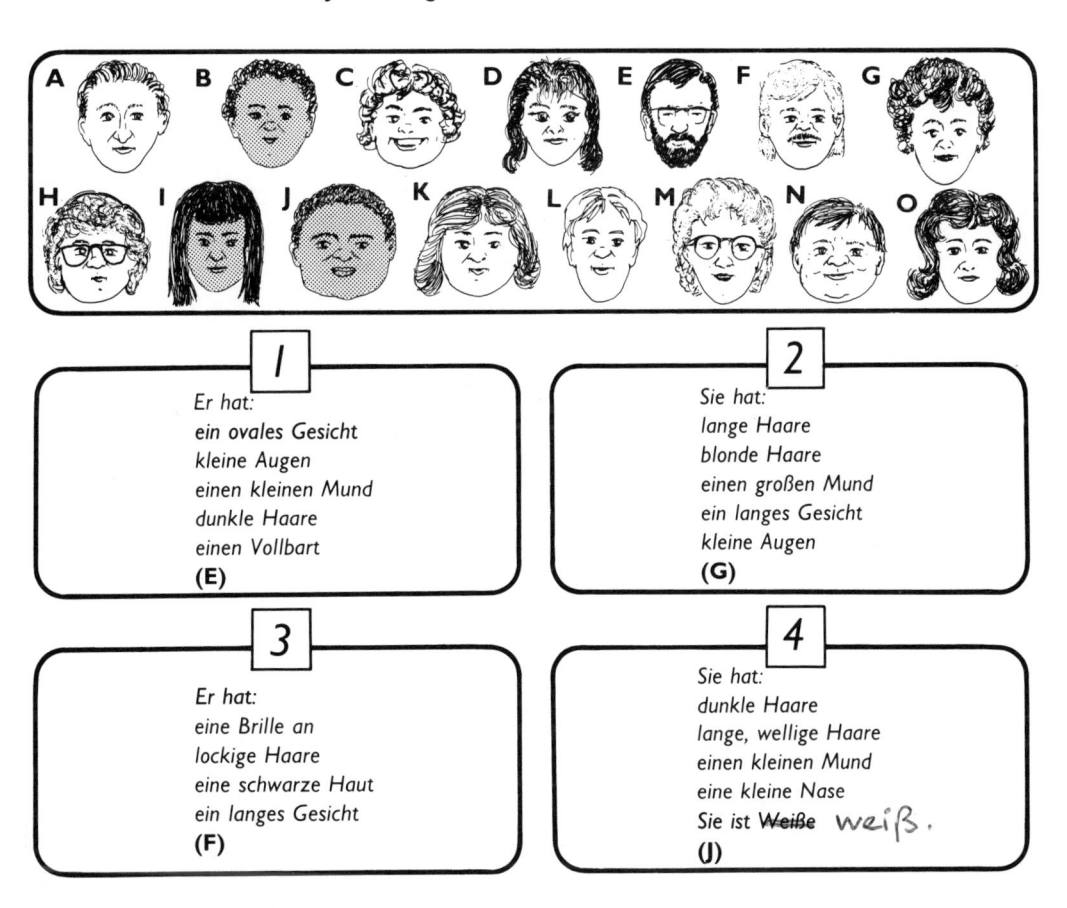

**1**
Er hat:
ein ovales Gesicht
kleine Augen
einen kleinen Mund
dunkle Haare
einen Vollbart
**(E)**

**2**
Sie hat:
lange Haare
blonde Haare
einen großen Mund
ein langes Gesicht
kleine Augen
**(G)**

**3**
Er hat:
eine Brille an
lockige Haare
eine schwarze Haut
ein langes Gesicht
**(F)**

**4**
Sie hat:
dunkle Haare
lange, wellige Haare
einen kleinen Mund
eine kleine Nase
Sie ist ~~Weiße~~ weiß.
**(J)**

# 1 PERSONAL IDENTIFICATION

### Exercise 2    Check the information

In this exercise one partner has information that is true (Wahr) and the other has information which may or may not be true (Wahr?) and which has to be checked. The partner who checks the information asks questions and makes notes of the correct information in his or her exercise book, to be written up later in full.

Zum Beispiel:   **A**   *Karla ist 13?*
                           **B**   *Ja.*
                           **A**   *Und ist sie schlank?*
                           **B**   *Nein. Sie ist rundlich.*
                           **A**   *Und sie hat lange, blonde Haare?*
                           **B**   *Neine. Sie hat kurze, blonde Haare.*
*usw.*

### 1
**Wahr**
*Ute*
*16*
*schlank*

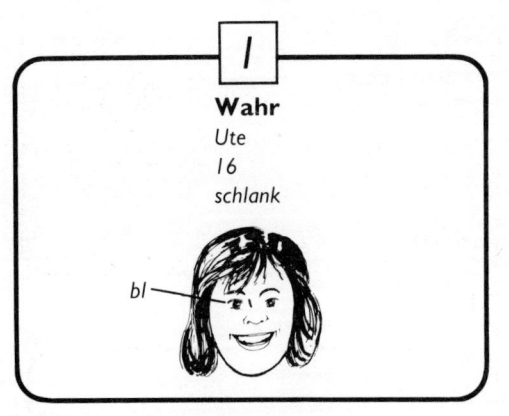

*bl*

### 2
**Wahr? Stell Fragen!**
*Manfred*
*32*
*dick*
*einen Vollbart*
*lange, wellige Haare*
*blonde Haare*
*ein langes Gesicht*
*eine Brille*

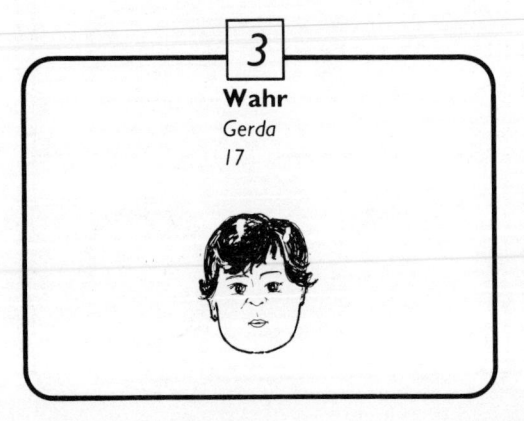

### 3
**Wahr**
*Gerda*
*17*

### 4
**Wahr? Stell Fragen!**
*Lutz*
*26*
*schlank*
*einen Schnurrbart*
*helle Haare*
*wellige, kurze Haare*
*braune Augen*
*eine kleine Nase*
*eine Brille*
*ein breites Gesicht*

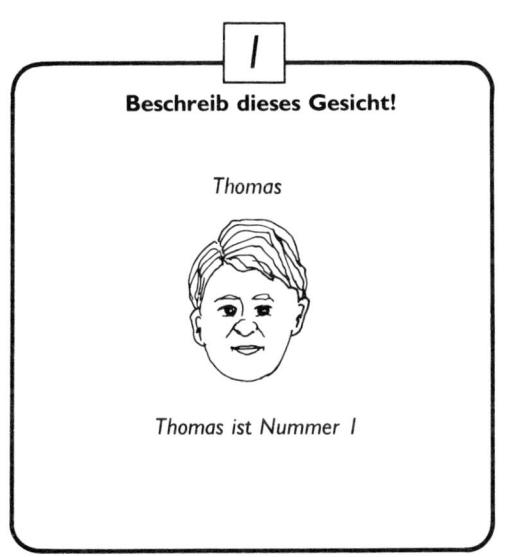

# 1 PERSONAL IDENTIFICATION

### Exercise 3  Describe the face

In this activity you describe a face to your partner, who identifies it from among the four faces he or she has. When the face has been identified, *both* partners write a description of it. Then your partner will describe a face for you to identify.

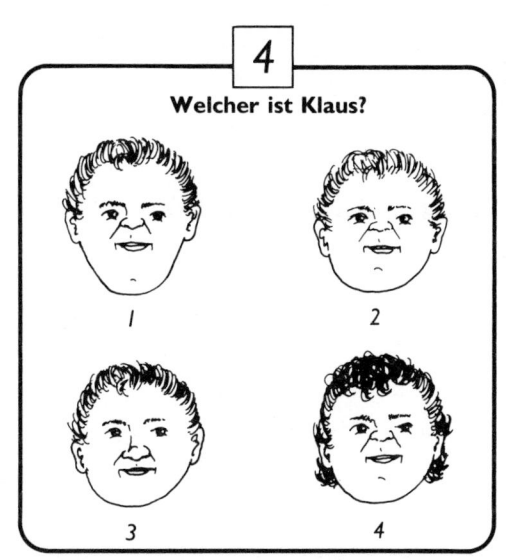

**1**

**Beschreib dieses Gesicht!**

Thomas

Thomas ist Nummer 1

**2**

**Welche ist Ute?**

**3**

**Beschreib dieses Gesicht!**

Inge

Inge ist Nummer 1

**4**

**Welcher ist Klaus?**

# 1 PERSONAL IDENTIFICATION

### Exercise 4   Draw the face

In this activity you and your partner take it in turns to describe a face. The person who is listening to the description draws the face. Compare the results with the originals.

**1** Beschreib dieses Gesicht!

**2** Beschreib dieses Gesicht!

**3** Beschreib dieses Gesicht!

**4** Beschreib dieses Gesicht!

**5** Beschreib dieses Gesicht!

**6** Beschreib dieses Gesicht!

**7** Beschreib dieses Gesicht!

**8** Beschreib dieses Gesicht!

# 1 PERSONAL IDENTIFICATION

### Exercise 5  What are you taking on holiday?

In this activity you tell each other some of the clothes you are taking on holiday with you. You take it in turns to identify the clothes being taken by making a note of the letter which is next to the item of clothing in the pictures below. When you have finished, the list of letters is read out and you and your partner will see whether they are right.
The list of clothes sometimes offers a choice of boys' or girls' wear.

Zum Beispiel:   A  Ich nehme zwei Paare Socken, einen Pulli, Shorts, eine Jeans, usw.
                B  Also. Du nimmst T, B, usw.

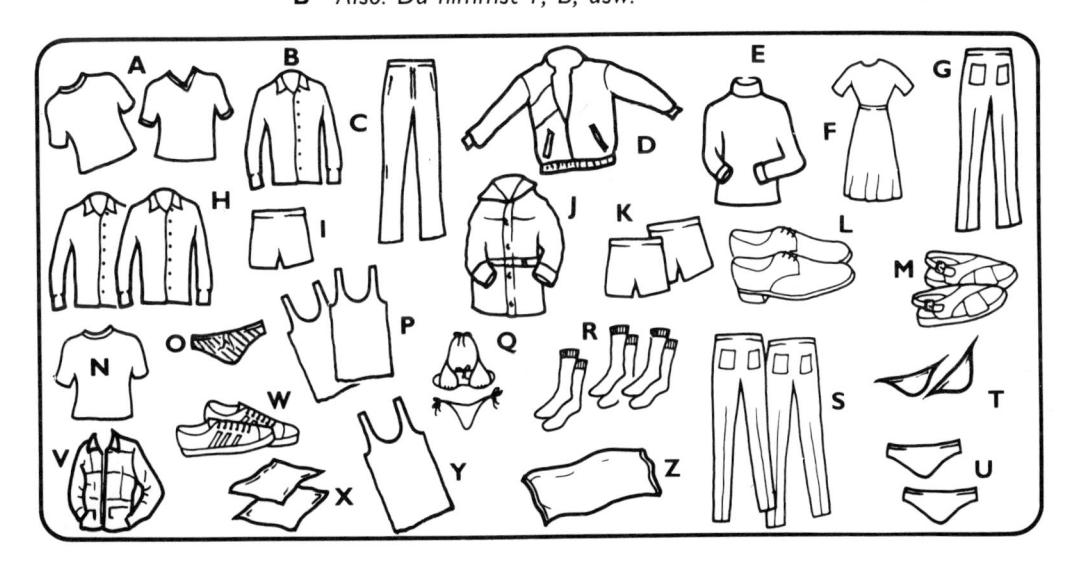

## 1

**Du nimmst folgendes mit**

| | |
|---|---|
| einen Regenmantel | J |
| einen Anorak | V |
| eine Hose | C |
| Socken | R |
| 2 Paare Unterhose | U  oder |
| 2 Slips | T |
| 2 T-Shirts | A |
| einen Pulli | E |
| Sandale | M |

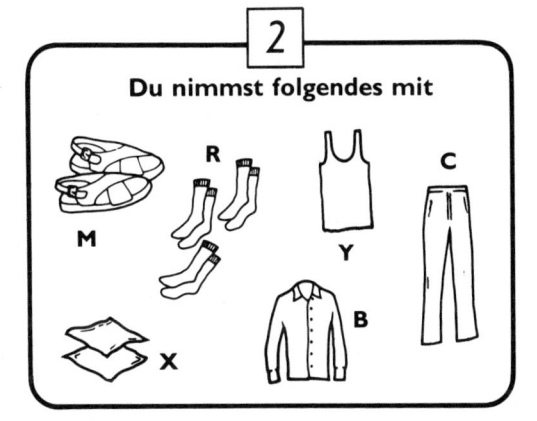

## 2

**Du nimmst folgendes mit**

M, R, Y, C, X, B

# 1 PERSONAL IDENTIFICATION

### Exercise 6   Packing

In this activity you and your partner tell each other all the clothes you each need to buy to take with you on holiday — you need to get a lot of things! The person listening makes a note of what is said and then checks back to see whether you have communicated accurately with each other. Then you both write out the shopping list.

Zum Beispiel:
- **A** Ich kaufe mir einen Rock, zwei T-Shirts, ein Paar Jeans, usw.
- **B** Also. Du kaufst dir einen Rock, ein T-Shirt . . .
- **A** Nein. Zwei T-Shirts.

usw.

**1** Ich kaufe mir

**2** Ich kaufe mir

**3** Ich kaufe mir

**4** Ich kaufe mir

**5** Ich kaufe mir

**6** Ich kaufe mir

# 1 PERSONAL IDENTIFICATION

### Exercise 7   Phoning ahead

Imagine that you are phoning Germany to say at what time your brother or sister or a friend will be arriving at a particular destination, so that the hosts can meet him or her and will know what he or she looks like. The partner who is listening should make a note of the description and then repeat it back. Remember that this is a role play of a telephone conversation.

*Zum Beispiel:*   **A**   *(Lifts phone) Schneider.*
**B**   *Hallo! Hier (gives name).*
**A**   *Ach! Hallo!*
**B**   *Alan ist schon unterwegs. Er kommt um 22 Uhr am Stuttgarter Hauptbahnhof an.*
**A**   *Gut. Um 22 Uhr.*
**B**   *Ja. Er trägt einen Pulli — einen blauen Pulli und eine Jeans.*
**A**   *Einen blauen Pulli und Jeans.*
**B**   *Ja. Er ist ziemlich groß und hat blonde Haare.*
**A**   *Ziemlich groß und er hat blonde Haare.*
     *Fein. In Ordnung. Danke schön für den Anruf.*
**B**   *Bitte sehr. Auf Wiederhören.*
**A**   *Auf Wiederhören.*

### 1
**Du rufst an!**
Claire
*Köln HBF*
*21.30*
*blue*
*yellow*

### 2
**Du rufst an!**
Steven
*Ulm HBF*
*20.30*
*black*

### 3
**Du rufst an!**
Helen
*Kassel HBF*
*14.15*
*blue*
*red*

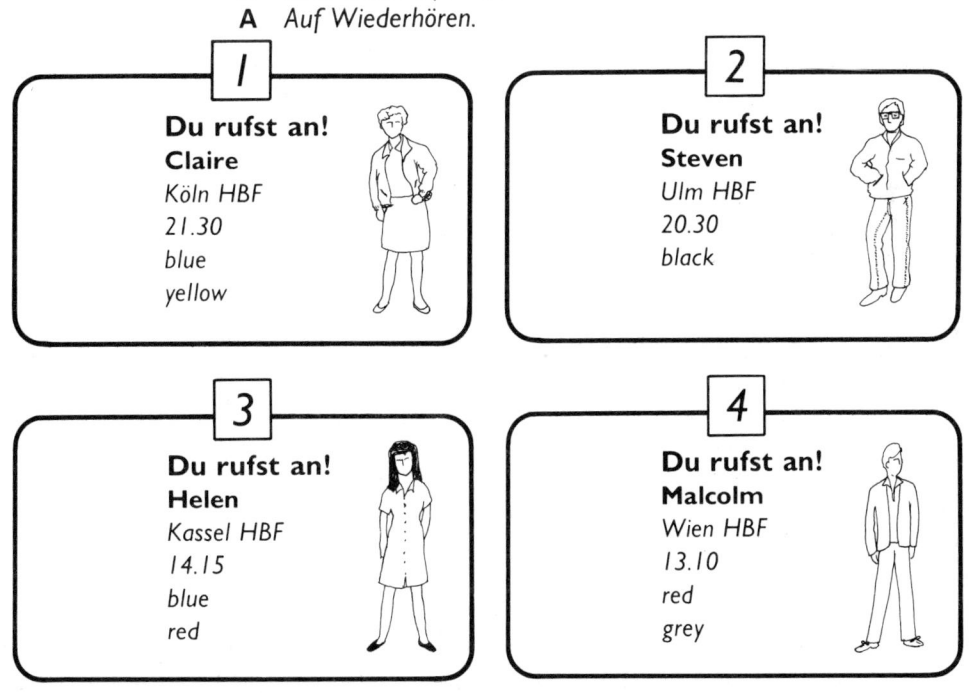

### 4
**Du rufst an!**
Malcolm
*Wien HBF*
*13.10*
*red*
*grey*

# 1 PERSONAL IDENTIFICATION

### Exercise 8  Check the facts

This activity is of the same type as Exercise 2 (*Wahr* or *Wahr*?)—you have to check information about someone. As you check the information, make notes and later write it up in full.

Zum Beispiel:
- **A** Also Karl ist 16?
- **B** Und wohnt in Hamburg?
- **A** Nein. Er wohnt in Kiel.
- **B** Mmm. Er hat lange, braune Haare?
- **A** Ja.
- **B** Und er ist 1,64 m groß?
- **A** Nein. Er ist 1,54 m.

usw.

### 1 Die Wahrheit
Tobias
Alter — 14
Größe — 1,60
Haare — lang, dunkel
Augen — blau
Wohnort — Bremen
Geschwister —
Haustiere — 0
Hobbys —

### 2 Ist das alles wahr?
Birgit
Alter — 17
Größe — 1,71
Haare — hell, glatt
Wohnort — Duisburg
Geschwister —
Haustiere —
Hobbys —

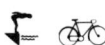

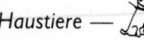

### 3 Die Wahrheit
Sven
Alter — 20
Größe — 1,68
Haare — kurz, schwarz
Schnurrbart
Augen — braun
Wohnort — Lübeck
Geschwister —
Haustiere — 
Hobbys —

### 4 Ist das alles wahr?
Barbara
Alter — 13
Größe — 1,51
Haare — braun, glatt, kurz
Augen — hellblau
Wohnort — Berlin
Geschwister —
Haustiere —
Hobbys —

# 2 LOCATION

### Exercise 1  Where does she live?

In this activity you and your partner take it in turns to give and obtain information about various people. In each case the person seeking the information must find out:
- address
- telephone number
- if he/she lives in a house or a flat
- where it is near.

Make notes about what you find out and then write it up later in full.

*Zum Beispiel:*
- **A** *Also Gabi. Wie ist ihre Adresse?*
- **B** *Königsstraße, 16.*
- **A** *Und wie ist ihre Telefonnummer?*
- **B** *Sie hat kein Telefon.*
- **A** *Wohnt sie in einem Haus oder in einem Wohnblock?*
- **B** *In einem Haus.*
- **A** *Und wo steht das Haus?*
- **B** *Nah am Museum.*

**Note:** To help you, the gender of the building referred to is shown as (m), (f) or (n). This will help you decide whether to say *nah am* or *nah an der*.

---

**1**

**Stell Fragen über Stefan!**
Adresse?
Telefonnummer?
Haus/Wohnblock?
Wo?

**Und dann stell Fragen über Georg, Kirsten, Frank und Ute!**

**Beantworte Fragen über Martina!**

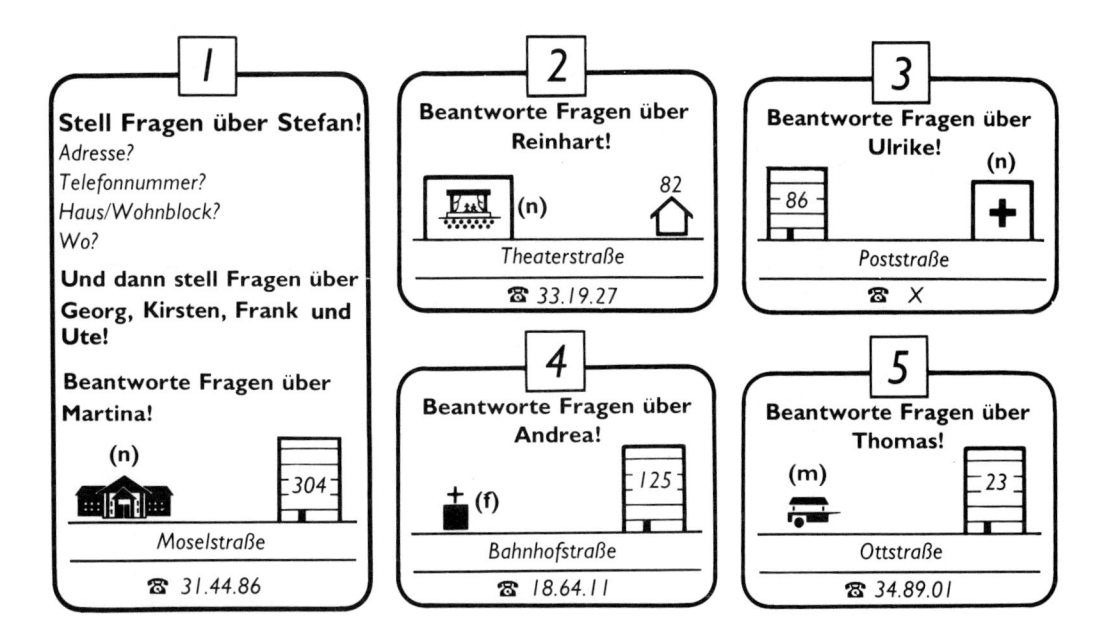

(n)   304
Moselstraße
☎ 31.44.86

---

**2**

**Beantworte Fragen über Reinhart!**

(n)   82
Theaterstraße
☎ 33.19.27

---

**3**

**Beantworte Fragen über Ulrike!**

86   (n)
Poststraße
☎ X

---

**4**

**Beantworte Fragen über Andrea!**

(f)   125
Bahnhofstraße
☎ 18.64.11

---

**5**

**Beantworte Fragen über Thomas!**

(m)   23
Ottstraße
☎ 34.89.01

# 2 LOCATION ..........................

### Exercise 2  Where does he live?

This activity is similar to Exercise 1, but more complicated. You have to take it in turns to find out the same four things (address, telephone number, if he or she lives in a house or flat and where it is) but on this occasion you must find out whether the person lives *near* the other building mentioned, whether he/she lives *opposite* it, or whether he/she lives directly *next* to it.
These three expressions are:

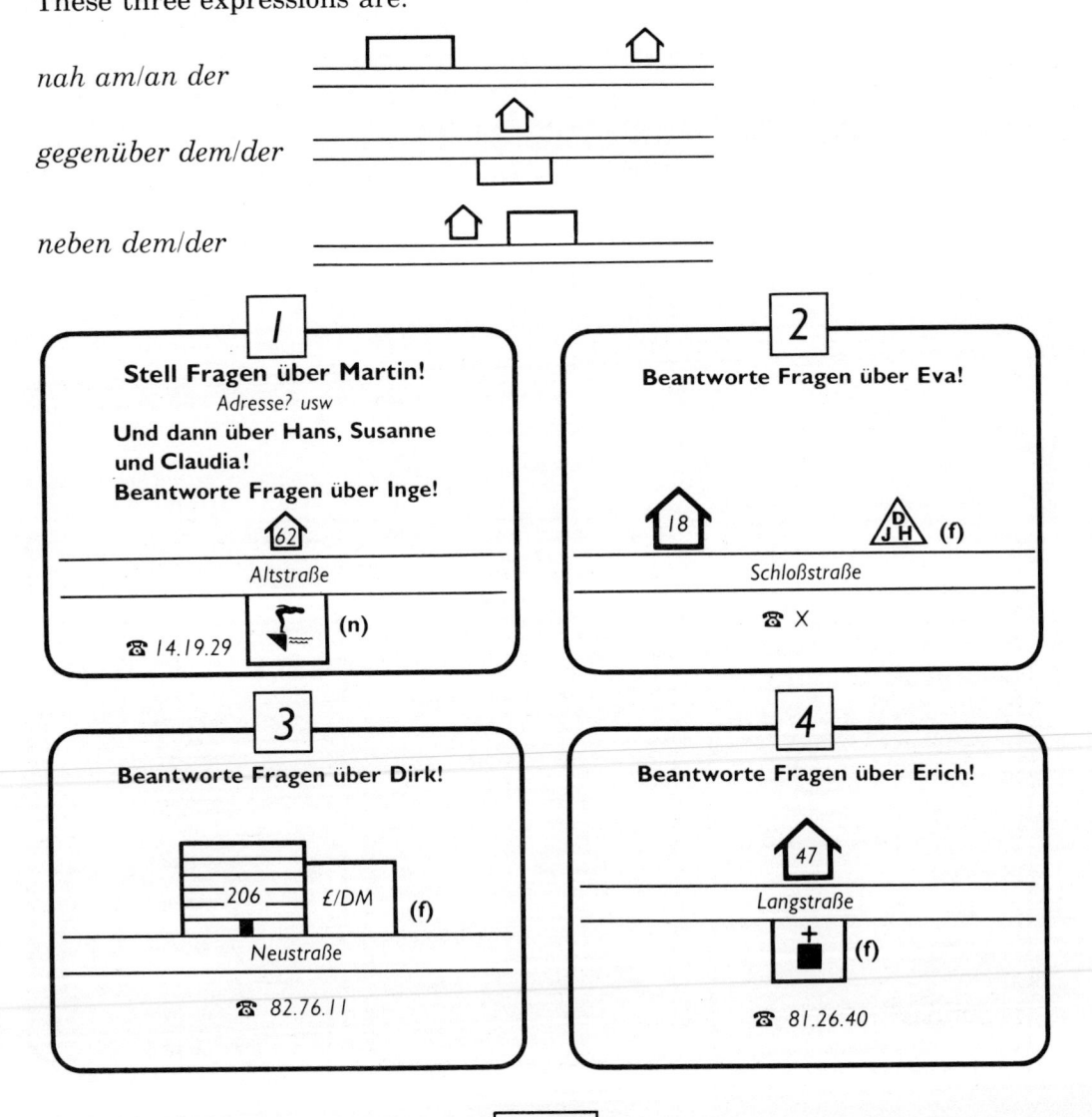

*nah am/an der*

*gegenüber dem/der*

*neben dem/der*

## 1
**Stell Fragen über Martin!**
*Adresse? usw*
**Und dann über Hans, Susanne und Claudia!**
**Beantworte Fragen über Inge!**

62
Altstraße

☎ 14.19.29   (n)

## 2
**Beantworte Fragen über Eva!**

18        D J H  (f)
Schloßstraße

☎ X

## 3
**Beantworte Fragen über Dirk!**

206  £/DM  (f)
Neustraße

☎ 82.76.11

## 4
**Beantworte Fragen über Erich!**

47
Langstraße

(f)

☎ 81.26.40

# 2 LOCATION

❏ *Exercise 3  Where do you live?*

In this activity you and your partner take it in turns to find out full details about where someone lives in Germany so that you could visit them and find their house easily.

You should find out:

    *Wohnort?* — the name of the place
    ✝? — where it is in Germany, and where it is near
    🏭/🏠? — whether it is a town or a village
    *A/T?* — address and telephone number
    *Standort?* — whereabouts their house is

❏     Zum Beispiel:
    **A** Wo wohnst du?
    **B** In Bleckede.
    **A** Wo liegt das?
    **B** In Norddeutschland. In der Nähe von Hamburg.
    **A** Ist das eine Stadt oder ein Dorf?
    **B** Ein Dorf.
    **A** Wie ist deine Adresse und deine Telefonnummer? (Kannst du mir deine Adresse geben?)
    **B** Ich wohne Ulmenstraße, 14. Meine Telefonnummer ist 0433 12.45.38.
    **A** Wo steht das Haus?
    **B** Nah am Jugendklub.

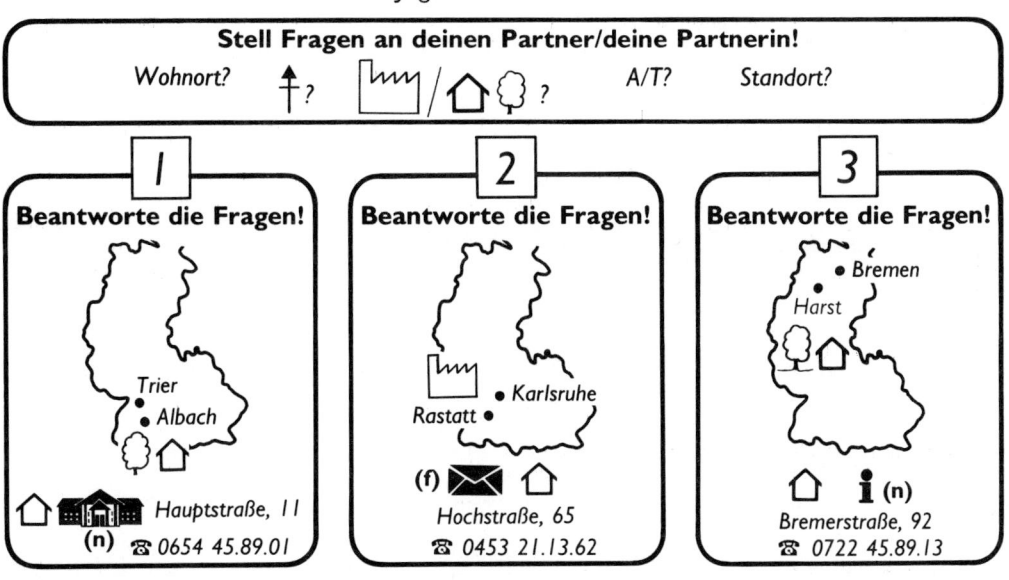

**Stell Fragen an deinen Partner/deine Partnerin!**

Wohnort?    ✝?    🏭/🏠?    A/T?    Standort?

---

**1**

**Beantworte die Fragen!**

Trier
• Albach

🏠 🏫 *Hauptstraße, 11*
**(n)** ☎ 0654 45.89.01

---

**2**

**Beantworte die Fragen!**

🏭 • Karlsruhe
Rastatt •

(f) ✉ 🏠
*Hochstraße, 65*
☎ 0453 21.13.62

---

**3**

**Beantworte die Fragen!**

• Bremen
Harst
🏠

🏠 ℹ (n)
*Bremerstraße, 92*
☎ 0722 45.89.13

# 3 FOOD AND QUANTITIES ....................

### Exercise 1    Test your partner

Study the list given below and when you have learnt the words, find a partner and test each other. You could take turns to ask five questions each. Keep a check of the number you get right.

Zum Beispiel:
- **A**  Nummer 6. Was ist das?
- **B**  (Das sind) Tomaten.
- **A**  Richtig. Und Nummer 10?
- **B**  Ich weiß nicht.
- **A**  Schinken.

| | | | | | |
|---|---|---|---|---|---|
| 1 | | grüner Salat | 15 | | Milch |
| 2 | | Bohnen | 16 | | Eier |
| 3 | | Bananen | 17 | | Brot |
| 4 | | Joghurt | 18 | | Salami |
| 5 | | Äpfel | 19 | | Käse |
| 6 | | Marmelade | 20 | | Apfelsinen |
| 7 | | Kaffee | 21 | | Karotten |
| 8 | | Erbsen | 22 | | Birnen |
| 9 | | Tomaten | 23 | | Schinken |
| 10 | | Kartoffeln | 24 | | Chips |
| 11 | | Würste | 25 | | Tee |
| 12 | | Salz | 26 | | Kekse |
| 13 | | Butter | 27 | | Limonade |
| 14 | | Sardinen | 28 | | Streichhölzer |

# 3 FOOD AND QUANTITIES

### Exercise 2  Good and bad ideas for a picnic

Imagine that you are going to have a picnic. Each of you has suggestions about what to get. Agree on the things to get and then write out the final list. In each dialogue say that you do not like something that your partner suggests, and do not forget to use expressions such as *Eine gute Idee* and *Ja, ich mag das*. etc.

Zum Beispiel:
- **A** Also. Für das Picknick. Was kaufen wir denn?
- **B** Grünen Salat.
- **A** Ja. Und Brot.
- **B** Ja. Brot natürlich. Und Streichhölzer.
- **A** Gute Idee. Und Sardinen.
- **B** Ach, nicht Sardinen. Ich mag Sardinen nicht.
- **A** OK.

**1 Deine Vorschläge**

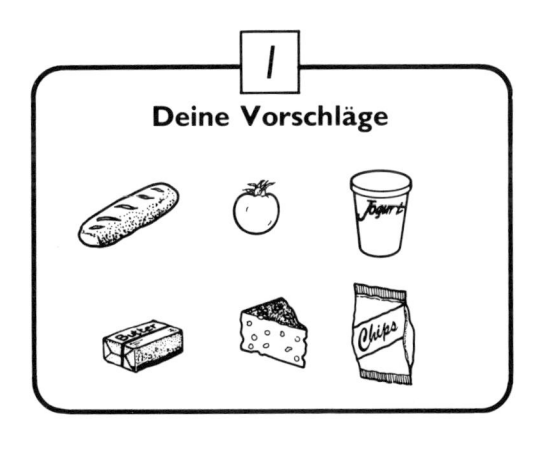

**2 Deine Vorschläge**

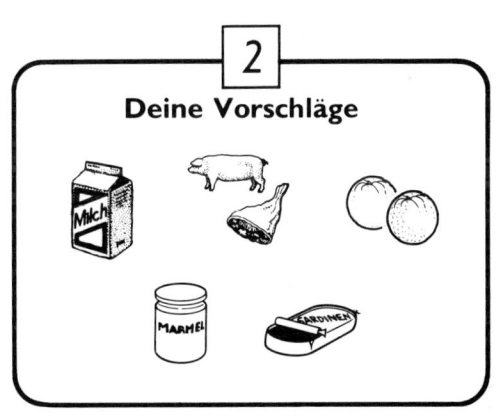

**3 Deine Vorschläge**

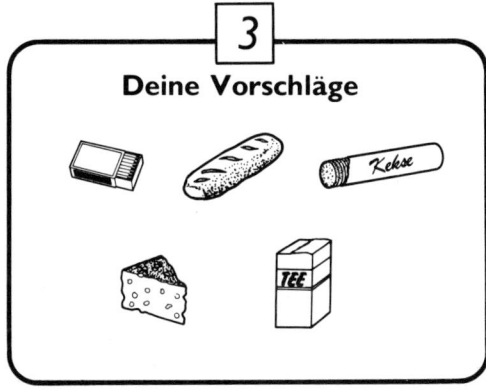

**4 Deine Vorschläge**

# 3 FOOD AND QUANTITIES

### Exercise 3   Quantities

In this activity one person reads out the quantities of various foods whilst the other picks out the correct picture from among the illustrations. The person who is listening then notes down the letter of the appropriate picture in his or her exercise book. At the end of each exercise you check to see whether the correct sequence of letters has been noted down. The partner who reads out the list of quantities has the correct sequence of letters so that he or she can check the partner's answers. Spell the letters out in German!

Don't forget 500 Gramm (g) = 1 Pfund (Pfd) = ½ Kilo (Kg)

**1**

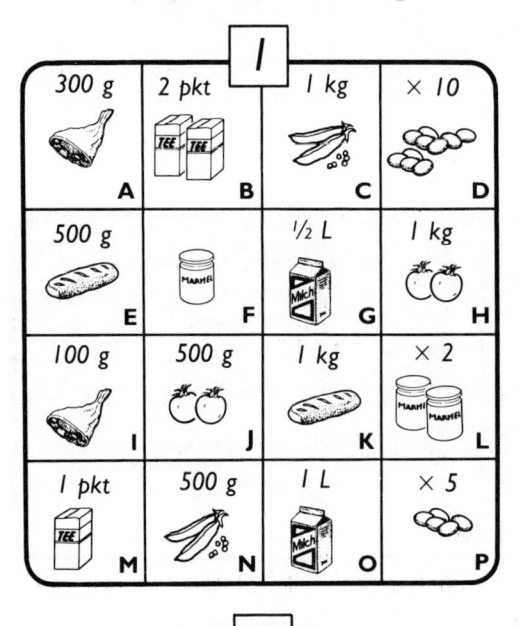

| 300 g (A) | 2 pkt (B) | 1 kg (C) | × 10 (D) |
| --- | --- | --- | --- |
| 500 g (E) | (F) | ½ L (G) | 1 kg (H) |
| 100 g (I) | 500 g (J) | 1 kg (K) | × 2 (L) |
| 1 pkt (M) | 500 g (N) | 1 L (O) | × 5 (P) |

**2**

250 g Kaffee
eine Dose Würste
zwei Pakete Chips
500 g Butter
1 Paket Nudeln
2 Kilo Äpfel
200 g Salami
2 Kilo Kartoffeln

N  F  J  A  H  L  P  I

**3**

1 Paket Kekse
100 g Salami
1 Glas Marmelade
2 Dosen Würste
3 Kilo Kartoffeln
1 Liter Limonade
200 g Käse
150 g Schinken

C  O  H  A  J  F  B  K

**4**

| 200 g (A) | × 1 (B) | 250 g (C) | 1 kg (D) |
| --- | --- | --- | --- |
| 1 kg (E) | 500 g (F) | 2 pkt (G) | 200 g (H) |
| 500 g (I) | 500 g (J) | 2 L (K) | 500 g (L) |
| 1 kg (M) | 3 pkt (N) | × 2 (O) | 1 L (P) |

# 3 FOOD AND QUANTITIES

❏ *Exercise 4   Taking down a shopping list*

Imagine that you are going to do some shopping for your German hosts. Your partner tells you what to get and you write notes as you are given the list. When you have noted the list your partner should check to see that you have written it down correctly.

You can make the notes in any way you like, but later, when you have checked it with your partner, write it out in full. Take it in turn to play the different roles.

❏   *Zum Beispiel:*   **A**   *Also. Hier ist die Liste.*
                           *Du kaufst ein Kilo Tomaten, usw.*

**Note:** eine Schachtel Streichhölzer
        zwei Schachteln Streichhölzer

### 1
**Die Liste**

½ kg Bohnen
1 kg Apfelsinen
2 Pakete Chips
250 g Käse
200 g Wurst
250 g Kaffee

### 2
**Die Liste**

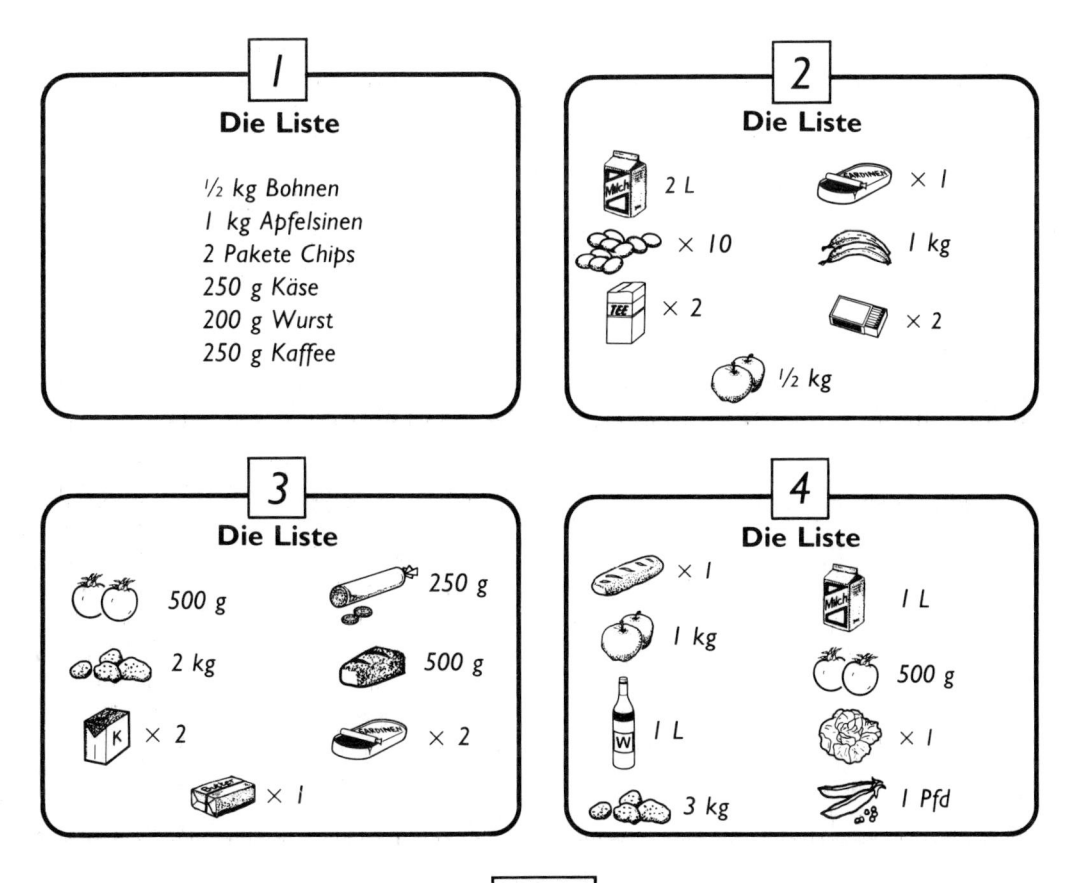

Milch 2 L
× 10
Tee × 2
× 1
1 kg
× 2
½ kg

### 3
**Die Liste**

500 g
2 kg
K × 2
250 g
500 g
× 2
× 1

### 4
**Die Liste**

× 1
1 kg
W 1 L
3 kg
1 L
500 g
× 1
1 Pfd

# 3 FOOD AND QUANTITIES

### Exercise 5   Shopping — how much to buy

Imagine that you have decided *what* to buy, but not the amounts. In the activity below, you each have suggestions to make about quantities to buy. As you get the suggested quantities from your partner note them down in your exercise book and then, when the list is complete, check with each other to see that you have communicated correctly.

*Zum Beispiel:*  **A**  Wieviel Schinken kaufen wir?
                **B**  250g. Und wieviele Tomaten?
                **A**  Ein halbes Pfund.

**Note:** eine Flasche Wein; zwei Flaschen Wein
       ein Liter Öl; ein halbes Liter Öl

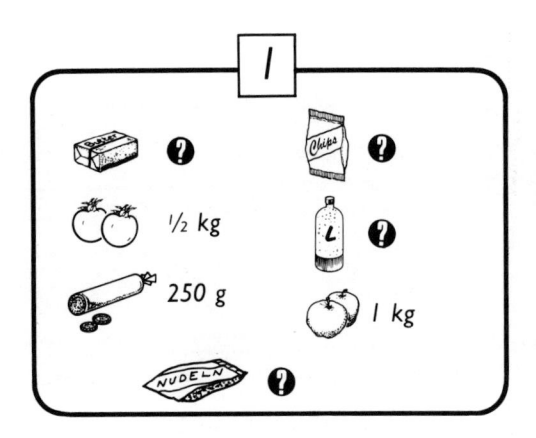

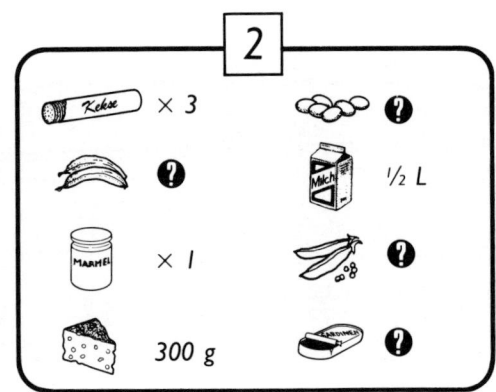

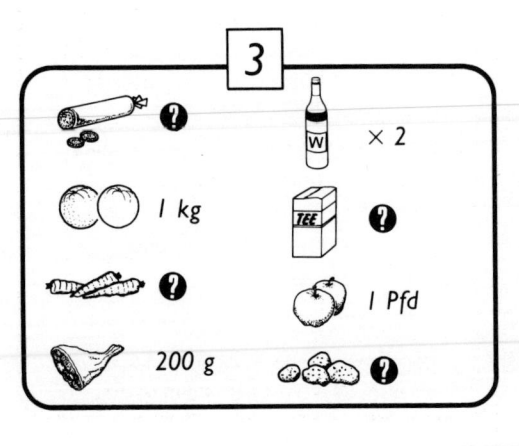

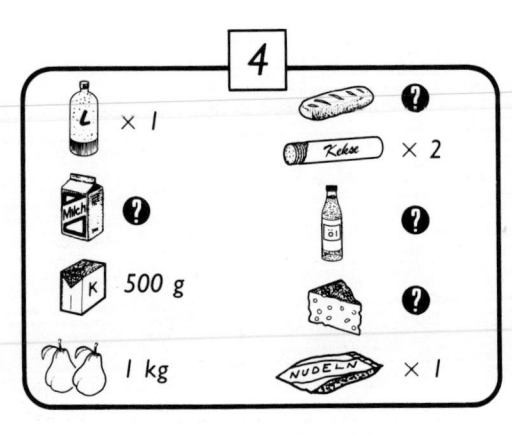

# 3 FOOD AND QUANTITIES

❏ *Exercise 6   Meals for the weekend*

Imagine that you are in Germany and are deciding what to eat over the weekend and that you are going to do the shopping on Friday for the next two days. You decide on the menus beforehand. Each of you has suggestions to make and, if you do not like the suggestions of your partner, you must say so and then make an alternative suggestion. Note the final suggestions for each meal in your exercise books. Remember these are German meals — so you might have cheese or cold meat for breakfast!
If you feel able to, you can make up the shopping list also, and to do that you need to work out the quantities you will need.

**Note:** Wie wäre es mit . . . ? How about . . . ?

❏   *Zum Beispiel:*   **A**   *Also, was essen wir am Samstag zum Frühstück?*
      **B**   *Eier und Brot.*
      **A**   *Ja. Und Kaffee.*
      **B**   *Und zu Mittag?*
      **A**   *Käse und Salami?*
      **B**   *Ja. Gute Idee. Und Brot auch.*
      **A**   *Und zu Abend?*
      **B**   *Fleisch?*
      **A**   *Nein. Ich mag Fleisch nicht. Wie wäre es mit Fisch?*
      *usw.*

## 1

**Deine Vorschläge**

|  | **Samstag** | **Sonntag** |
|---|---|---|
| Frühstück | Tee<br>Marmelade | Käse |
| Mittagessen | Fleisch<br>Äpfel | Pommes Frites<br>Erbsen |
| Abendessen | Brot<br>Tee<br>Limonade | Tomatensalat<br>Wurst |

## 2

**Deine Vorschläge**

|  | **Samstag** | **Sonntag** |
|---|---|---|
| Frühstück | Kaffee<br>Käse | Bananen<br>Kaffee |
| Mittagessen | Wurst<br>Birnen | Omelette<br>mit Käse |
| Abendessen | Nudelnsalat | Fleisch<br>Kartoffeln |

**Now do one yourselves —
a menu for the weekend.**

# 4 SHOPS AND SHOPPING

📎 *Exercise 1   The shops*

Test each other once you have studied the symbols.

📎    *Zum Beispiel:*   **A**  Nummer 3.
   **B**  Die Metzgerei.
   **A**  Richtig.
   **B**  Nummer 6.
   usw.

1   die Metzgerei
2   die Bäckerei
3   die Apotheke
4   £/DM   die Bank
5   die Post
6   der Markt
7   der Supermarkt
8   das Café
9   der Gemüsehändler

# 4 SHOPS AND SHOPPING

**Exercise 2** *Where are they going and why?*

With your partner work out which shops people are going to and what they want to buy. Make a note of the answers and write the information up as follows:

Markus geht zur Bank, um einen Scheck für 200 DM einzulösen.

*Zum Beispiel:*
- **A** *Wohin geht Markus?*
- **B** *Er geht zur Bank. Warum geht er zur Bank?*
- **A** *Er will einen Scheck für 200 DM einlösen. (Um einen Scheck für 200 DM einzulösen.)*
  *Und Ulrike. Wohin geht sie?*
- **B** *Sie geht zur Apotheke. Warum?*
- **A** *Sie will Schmerztabletten kaufen. (Um Schmerztabletten zu kaufen.)*

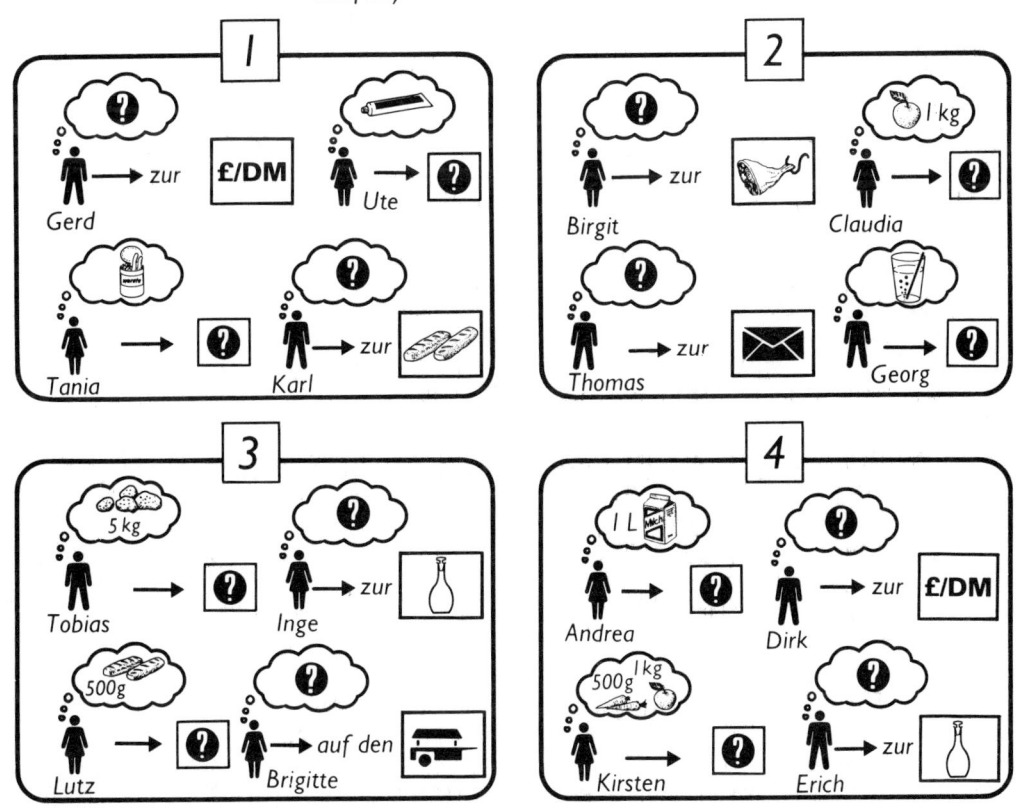

# 4 SHOPS AND SHOPPING ....................

### Exercise 3  At the shops

In this activity you practise buying things. One partner plays the part of the shopkeeper and does the simple addition to tell the other partner who is playing the part of the customer how much to pay.

*Zum Beispiel:*  **A**  *Guten Tag.*
　　　　　　　　**B**  *Guten Tag. Was wäre es?*
　　　　　　　　**A**  *500 g Tomaten, bitte.*
　　　　　　　　**B**  *Danke. 0.80 DM, bitte. Sonst noch etwas?*
　　　　　　　　**A**  *Ja. Einen grünen Salat.*
　　　　　　　　**B**  *Ein Salat. 0.50 DM. Das macht 1.30 DM, bitte.*
　　　　　　　　**A**  *1.30 DM.*
　　　　　　　　**B**  *Danke schön. Auf Wiedersehen.*
　　　　　　　　**A**  *Auf Wiedersehen.*

**1  In der Bäckerei**
*Du willst folgendes kaufen:*
500 g Graubrot

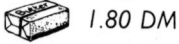

**2  Im Lebensmittelgeschäft**
0.78 DM 
1.80 DM
1.20 DM 

**3  Auf dem Markt**
*Du willst folgendes kaufen:*
1 kg 🍎 
5 kg 🥔

**4  Im Lebensmittelgeschäft**
1 L  0.99 DM
250 g  1.35 DM
5.40 DM 

**5  Auf der Post**
*Du willst folgendes kaufen:*
3 ×  1.20   2 × 1.40

**6  Auf der Markt**
1 kg  2.30 DM       500 g  1.10 DM 
1 kg  1.60 DM       500 g  0.90 DM

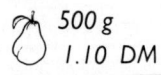

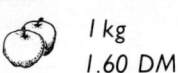

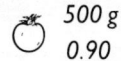

# 4 SHOPS AND SHOPPING

❏ Exercise 4   At the post office

(a) First a test on countries— learn the words and then test each other.

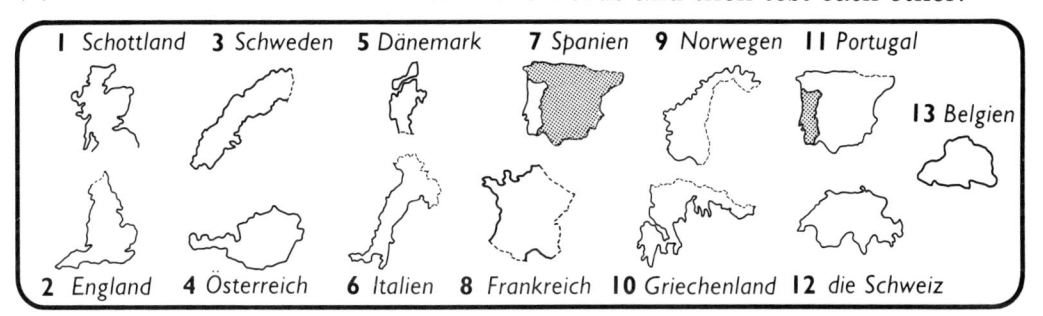

| 1 Schottland | 3 Schweden | 5 Dänemark | 7 Spanien | 9 Norwegen | 11 Portugal |
|---|---|---|---|---|---|
| | | | | | 13 Belgien |
| 2 England | 4 Österreich | 6 Italien | 8 Frankreich | 10 Griechenland | 12 die Schweiz |

(b) In this activity you practise asking for stamps so that you can send letters and postcards to various destinations.
The exercises are in two parts — you first find out where people are on holiday and you note this information down. Then you find out from your partner the cost of stamps for a letter or a card to some of your friends.

❏   *Zum Beispiel:*
   *Erster Teil*
   **A**   Wo ist Inge?
   **B**   Sie ist in der Schweiz. Und wo ist Karl?
   **A**   Er ist in Griechenland.
   usw.

   *Zweiter Teil*
   **A**   Was kostet ein Brief in die Schweiz?
   **B**   0.80 DM. Und nach Griechenland?
   **A**   0.90 DM.
   usw.

## 1
**Wo sind sie?**

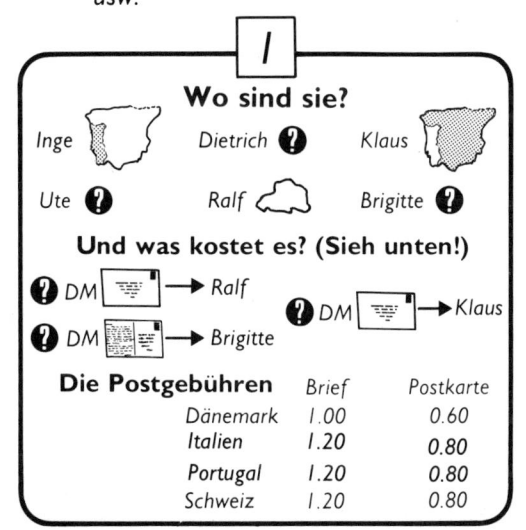

Inge    Dietrich ❓   Klaus
Ute ❓   Ralf    Brigitte ❓

**Und was kostet es? (Sieh unten!)**

❓ DM ✉ → Ralf
❓ DM ✉ → Klaus
❓ DM ▦ → Brigitte

**Die Postgebühren**

| | Brief | Postkarte |
|---|---|---|
| Dänemark | 1.00 | 0.60 |
| Italien | 1.20 | 0.80 |
| Portugal | 1.20 | 0.80 |
| Schweiz | 1.20 | 0.80 |

## 2
**Wo sind sie?**

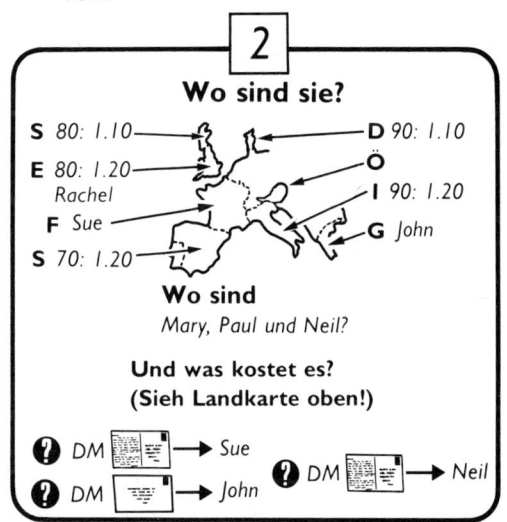

S 80: 1.10 ——————— D 90: 1.10
E 80: 1.20 ——————— Ö
Rachel
F  Sue ———————— I 90: 1.20
S 70: 1.20 ——————— G  John

**Wo sind**
Mary, Paul und Neil?

**Und was kostet es?**
**(Sieh Landkarte oben!)**

❓ DM ▦ → Sue
❓ DM ✉ → John
❓ DM ▦ → Neil

# 5 TRAVEL BY BUS AND TRAM ..............

*Exercise 1    Destinations*

In this activity you learn how to say your destination on a bus route. Study the list and then test your partner by covering the words and asking questions in the way shown below.

*Zum Beispiel:*   **A**  *Wohin fährt die Linie 8?*
  **B**  *Zum Bahnhof.*
  **A**  *Ja. Richtig.*
  **B**  *Wohin fährt die Linie 12?*
  **A**  *Zur ... zum ... ich weiß nicht.*
  **A**  *Zum Schloß. Wohin fährt die Linie 8?*
  *usw.*

| Linie | | Reiseziel | Linie | | Reiseziel |
|---|---|---|---|---|---|
| 4 |  | zum Schloß | 20 |  | zum Krankenhaus |
| 6 |  | zum Dom | 21 | DB | zum Bahnhof |
| 7 |  | zur Jugendherberge | 23 |  | zum Marktplatz |
| 9 |  | zum Rathaus | 25 |  | zum Informationsbüro |
| 10 |  | zum Museum | 26 |  | zum See |
| 11 | TECKSDORF | nach Tecksdorf | 28 | CITY | zur Stadtmitte |
| 13 |  | zum Schwimmbad | 32 | ZOO | zum Zoo |
| 14 |  | zum Park | 36 |  | zur Post |
| 16 |  | zum Stadion | 41 | BREBACH | nach Brebach |
| 19 |  | zum Campingplatz | | | |

# 5 TRAVEL BY BUS AND TRAM

❏ *Exercise 2    Which bus or tram route?*

In this activity you find out from each other the various bus and tram routes to different destinations. Note the answers in your exercise books and check after each exercise to see whether you have passed on the information correctly.

❏ *Zum Beispiel:*  **A**  Welcher Bus fährt zum Stadion?
  **B**  Die Linie 8. Und welche Straßenbahn fährt nach Esch?
  **A**  Die Linie 29.
  usw.

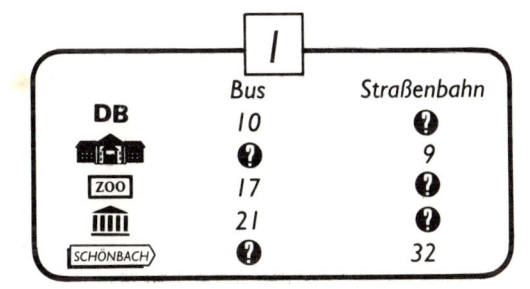

### 1
| | Bus | Straßenbahn |
|---|---|---|
| DB | 10 | ❓ |
| 🏠 | ❓ | 9 |
| ZOO | 17 | ❓ |
| 🏛 | 21 | ❓ |
| SCHÖNBACH | ❓ | 32 |

### 2
| | Bus | Straßenbahn |
|---|---|---|
| JH | 11 | ❓ |
| ↵ | ❓ | 9 |
| DB WENDEL | 23 | ❓ |
| | ❓ | 16 |
| 🏛 | 78 | ❓ |

### 3
| | Bus | Straßenbahn |
|---|---|---|
| 🌳🌳 | 66 | ❓ |
| ALTENKESSEL | ❓ | 14 |
| ✚ | 3 | ❓ |
| C | ❓ | 19 |
| | ❓ | 22 |

### 4
| | Bus | Straßenbahn |
|---|---|---|
| 🚃 | ❓ | 3 |
| NAUBERG | 32 | ❓ |
| i | 6 | ❓ |
| ⛵ | ❓ | 14 |
| CITY | 7 | ❓ |

### 5
| | Bus | Straßenbahn |
|---|---|---|
| 📯 | 23 | ❓ |
| ✚ | ❓ | 5 |
| BOLTHEIM | ❓ | 40 |
| 🏛 | 22 | ❓ |
| i | ❓ | 35 |

### 6
| | Bus | Straßenbahn |
|---|---|---|
| 🏰 | ❓ | 44 |
| HOMBURG | ❓ | 15 |
| 🌳🌳 | 37 | ❓ |
| ⛵ | ❓ | 9 |
| JH | 55 | ❓ |

# 5 TRAVEL BY BUS AND TRAM

❏ *Exercise 3    Where is the bus stop you want?*

In this exercise you find out where the stop is for a particular bus or tram route. Note the answer which your partner gives you and then later write it up as follows:

   Die Haltestelle für die Linie 8 ist am Dom in der Mainzerstraße.

If you are not sure how to write a word, ask your partner to spell the word to you in German.

❏    *Zum Beispiel:*    **A**    Wo ist die Bushaltestelle für die Linie 8, bitte?
                       **B**    Am Informationsbüro in der Karlstraße.

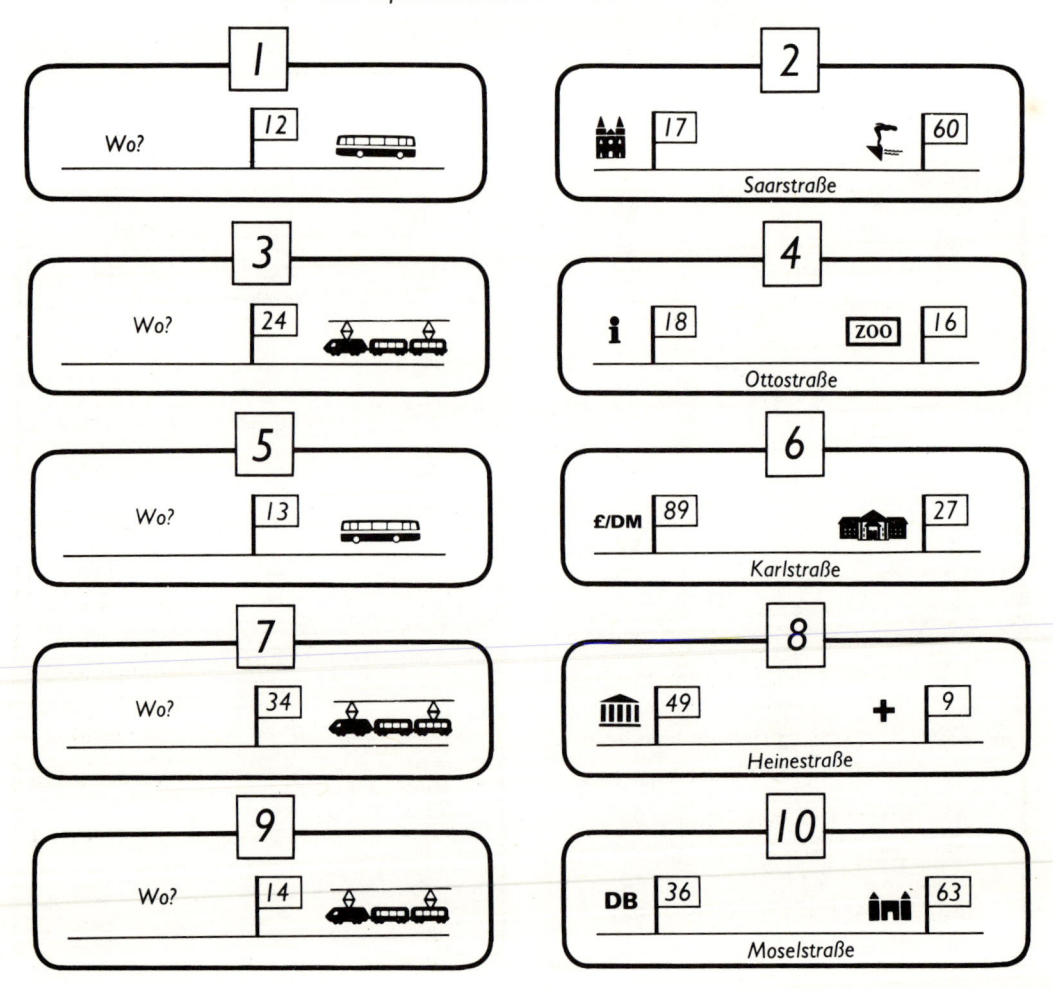

**1**  Wo? 12 🚌

**2**  ⛪ 17   ⚓ 60   Saarstraße

**3**  Wo? 24 🚋

**4**  i 18   ZOO 16   Ottostraße

**5**  Wo? 13 🚌

**6**  £/DM 89   🏛 27   Karlstraße

**7**  Wo? 34 🚋

**8**  🏛 49   ✚ 9   Heinestraße

**9**  Wo? 14 🚋

**10**  DB 36   🏨 63   Moselstraße

26

# 5 TRAVEL BY BUS AND TRAM

**Exercise 4** Which bus is it and where is the stop?

In this activity you take turns to ask each other:
  a) which route goes to a particular destination
  b) where the bus or tram stop is.

Each of you has a series of questions to ask and each of you has a panel of information so that you can answer your partner's questions.

Note the answers and then check back later with your partner.

Zum Beispiel:  **A**  Welcher Bus (Welche Straßenbahn) fährt zum See?
  **B**  Die Linie 8.
  **A**  Und wo ist die Haltestelle, bitte?
  **B**  Am Dom.
  usw.

Remember in your answer that it can be *am* or *an der*.

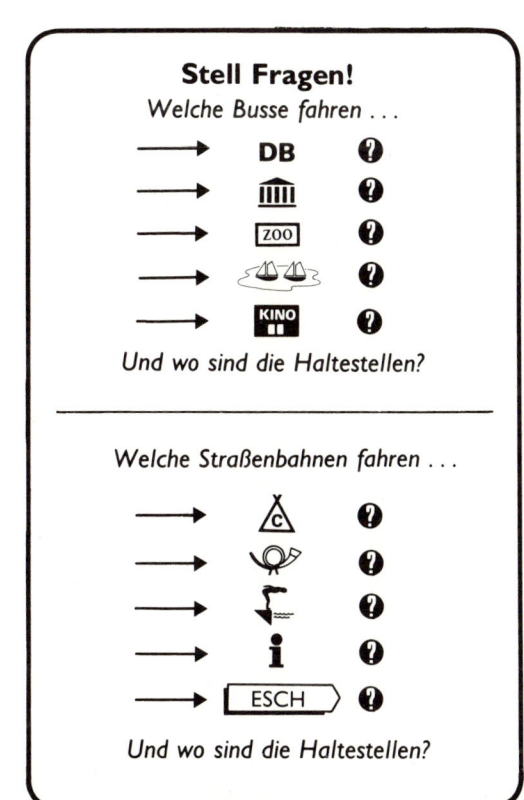

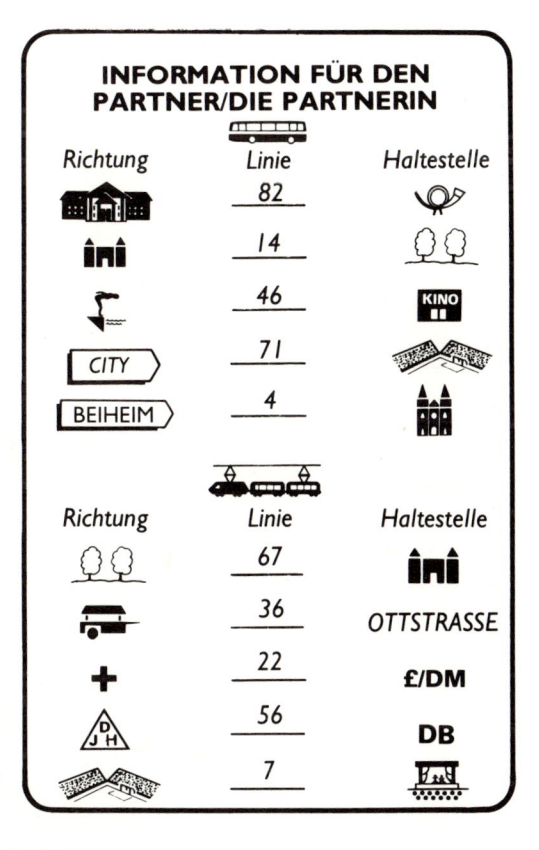

### Stell Fragen!

Welche Busse fahren . . .

→ DB ?
→ 🏛 ?
→ ZOO ?
→ ⛵ ?
→ KINO ?

Und wo sind die Haltestellen?

---

Welche Straßenbahnen fahren . . .

→ 🔺C ?
→ 📯 ?
→ 🏭 ?
→ i ?
→ ESCH ?

Und wo sind die Haltestellen?

### INFORMATION FÜR DEN PARTNER/DIE PARTNERIN

| Richtung | Linie | Haltestelle |
|---|---|---|
| 🏛 | 82 | 📯 |
| 🏨 | 14 | 🌳🌳 |
| 🏭 | 46 | KINO |
| CITY | 71 | ⛵ |
| BEIHEIM | 4 | 🏰 |

| Richtung | Linie | Haltestelle |
|---|---|---|
| 🌳🌳 | 67 | 🏨 |
| 🚐 | 36 | OTTSTRASSE |
| ✚ | 22 | £/DM |
| DJH | 56 | DB |
| ⛵ | 7 | 🏛 |

27

# 5 TRAVEL BY BUS AND TRAM ................

### Exercise 5  How do I get there and where do I get off?

In this activity you take it in turns to ask your partner how to reach certain places by bus and where you need to get off. Make a note of the information and then check back later to see whether you understood the information correctly.

Zum Beispiel:
- **A** Welcher Bus fährt zum Schloß, bitte?
- **B** Die Linie 6.
- **B** Und wo steigt man aus?
- **A** An der Marienstraße.

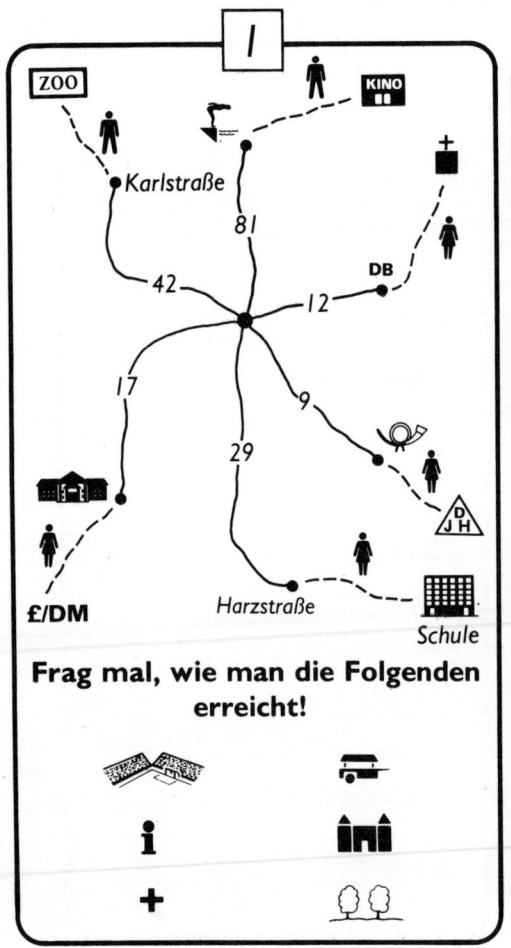

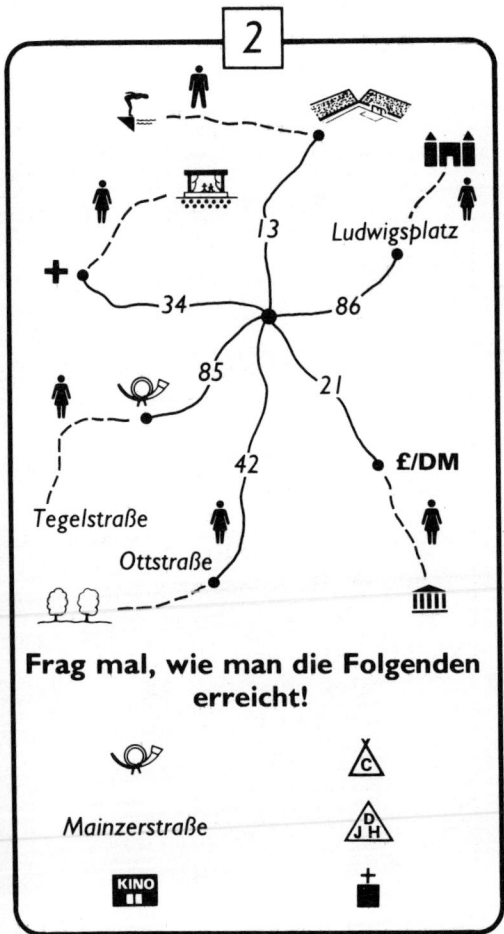

## 1

(Karlstraße, Harzstraße, Schule, ZOO, KINO, DB, £/DM; Linien 81, 42, 12, 17, 9, 29)

**Frag mal, wie man die Folgenden erreicht!**

## 2

(Ludwigsplatz, Tegelstraße, Ottstraße, Mainzerstraße, KINO, £/DM; Linien 13, 34, 86, 85, 42, 21)

**Frag mal, wie man die Folgenden erreicht!**

# 6 TRAVEL BY TRAIN

❏ **Exercise 1  Train times and platforms**

In this activity you take it in turns to find out the departure times of trains and the platforms they leave from. Note down the time and the platform number.

❏ Zum Beispiel:
- **A** Wann fährt der nächste Zug nach Bonn, bitte?
- **B** 18.56.
- **A** Und wo fährt er ab? (Auf welchem Gleis fährt er ab?)
- **B** Gleis 9.

### FAHRPLAN

| Richtung | Abfahrt | Gleis |
|---|---|---|
| Düsseldorf | 09.30 | 4 |
| Hamburg | 10.21 | 1 |
| Paris | 09.47 | 3 |
| München | 12.17 | 8 |
| Genf | 11.04 | 2 |
| Trier | 08.55 | 9 |
| Augsburg | 07.38 | 7 |
| Koblenz | 10.12 | 16 |
| Kiel | 11.25 | 5 |
| Freiburg | 09.17 | 2 |

**Frag mal, wann folgende Züge abfahren!**

Kassel                Gleis?
Frankfurt
Stuttgart
Wien
Münster
Würzburg
Köln
Karlsruhe
Bremen
Lübeck

# 6 TRAVEL BY TRAIN

◆ Exercise 2  When does it leave and when does it arrive?

In this activity you take it in turns to find out departure and arrival times of trains. Note down the times in each case and check back later with your partner to see whether you have communicated properly.

◆ Zum Beispiel: **A** Wann fährt der nächste Zug nach Bern?
**B** Um 18.15.
**A** Danke. Und wann kommt er (in Bern) an?
**B** Um 16.35.

### FAHRPLAN

| Abfahrt | Richtung | Ankunft |
|---------|----------|---------|
| 09.20 | Mainz | 09.53 |
| 10.25 | Koblenz | 11.11 |
| 09.16 | Köln | 10.45 |
| 11.18 | Hannover | 13.24 |
| 12.04 | München | 16.00 |
| 10.30 | Freiburg | 13.58 |
| 11.06 | Kassel | 13.34 |
| 08.55 | Bremen | 11.50 |
| 09.40 | Saarbrücken | 11.26 |
| 11.23 | Stuttgart | 13.10 |

### Frag mal um Auskunft!

Bonn   ab?   an?
Trier
Düsseldorf
Würzburg
Basel
Kiel
Regensburg
Wiesbaden
Münster
Augsburg

# 6 TRAVEL BY TRAIN

### Exercise 3  Train times, platforms and tickets

In this activity you take it in turns to ask your partner for train times, the departure platform for the train and then for a ticket. The tickets are shown as follows:

   zweimal einfach — 2 × →
   einmal hin und zurück — 1 × ⇌

Make a note of the times, the platform and the cost of the ticket and check later with your partner to see whether the communication was successful.

Zum Beispiel:  
A  Wann fährt der nächste Zug nach Freiburg?  
B  14.34.  
A  Wo fährt er ab?  
B  Gleis 4.  
A  Dreimal hin und zurück, bitte.  
B  Dreimal hin und zurück. 24 DM, bitte.  
A  Danke sehr.  
B  Bitte schön.

**1**
**Beamte/Beamtin**
Bremen 14.23
Gleis 8
2 × → = 60.00 DM
2 × ⇌ = 110.00 DM

**2**
**Reisende**
→ München?
Gleis?
1 × ⇌

**3**
**Beamte/Beamtin**
Münster 14.05
Gleis 5
3 × → = 30.00 DM
3 × ⇌ = 56.00 DM

**4**
**Reisende**
→ Bonn?
Gleis?
2 × →

**5**
**Beamte/Beamtin**
Hamburg 18.29
Gleis 14
1 × → = 30.00 DM
1 × ⇌ = 54.00 DM

**6**
**Reisende**
→ Kassel?
Gleis?
2 × ⇌

# 6 TRAVEL BY TRAIN

### Exercise 4  Timetables

In this activity you have to complete a train timetable by asking your partner for the necessary details. First make yourself a blank timetable grid, then fill it in by asking your partner the appropriate questions. When you have finished, check with the original to see how you have done. Then your partner has a go and you provide the answers from the information you have.

Zum Beispiel:
- **A** Also, der erster Zug. Wann fährt er ab?
- **B** Um 12.34.
- **A** Und wohin fährt er?
- **B** Nach Trier.
- **A** Wann kommt er an?
- **B** Um 13.10.

usw.

### 1
**FAHRPLAN**

| Abfahrt | Richtung | Ankunft | Gleis |
|---------|----------|---------|-------|
| 10.20 | Bonn | 11.40 | 6 |
| 11.05 | Düsseldorf | 13.10 | 3 |
| 09.50 | Mainz | 10.32 | 12 |
| 10.36 | Köln | 12.35 | 13 |

### 2
**FAHRPLAN**

| Abfahrt | Richtung | Ankunft | Gleis |
|---------|----------|---------|-------|
| 18.10 | Kiel | 18.35 | 9 |
| 17.56 | Essen | 18.31 | 10 |
| 17.49 | Dortmund | 18.53 | 17 |
| 19.02 | Krefeld | 19.49 | 2 |

### 3
**FAHRPLAN**

| Abfahrt | Richtung | Ankunft | Gleis |
|---------|----------|---------|-------|
| 14.16 | Bremen | 16.40 | 2 |
| 13.50 | Bremerhaven | 16.22 | 4 |
| 14.22 | Hamburg | 16.18 | 7 |
| 13.56 | Emden | 15.46 | 11 |

# 7 THE YOUTH HOSTEL ......................

### Exercise 1   Rooms in the youth hostel

Study the words and symbols given below, and when you have learnt them, find a partner and test each other.

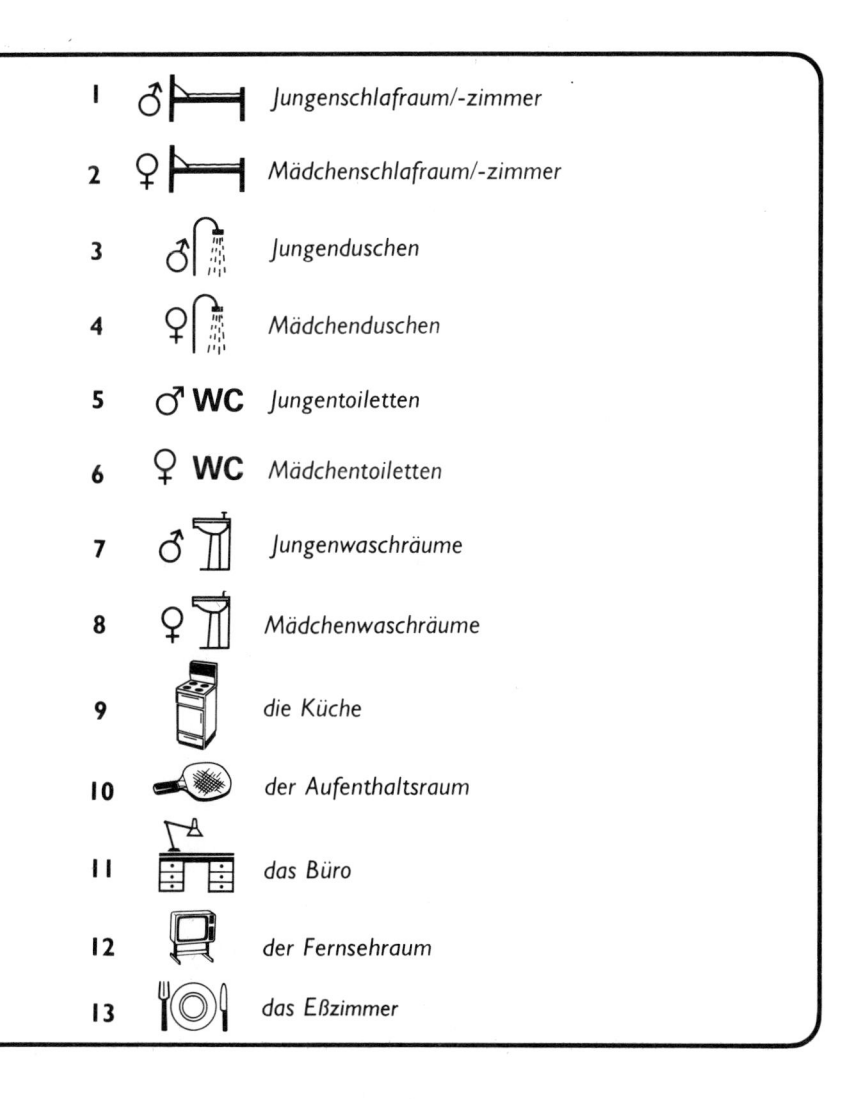

| | | |
|---|---|---|
| 1 | ♂🛏 | Jungenschlafraum/-zimmer |
| 2 | ♀🛏 | Mädchenschlafraum/-zimmer |
| 3 | ♂🚿 | Jungenduschen |
| 4 | ♀🚿 | Mädchenduschen |
| 5 | ♂ WC | Jungentoiletten |
| 6 | ♀ WC | Mädchentoiletten |
| 7 | ♂🚰 | Jungenwaschräume |
| 8 | ♀🚰 | Mädchenwaschräume |
| 9 | 🍳 | die Küche |
| 10 | 🏸 | der Aufenthaltsraum |
| 11 | 🗄 | das Büro |
| 12 | 📺 | der Fernsehraum |
| 13 | 🍽 | das Eßzimmer |

# 7 THE YOUTH HOSTEL ........................

❏ *Exercise 2   Where the rooms are*

In this activity you take it in turns to tell your partner where the rooms are in a youth hostel. One of you has a diagram of where the rooms are and the other, who draws an outline of the youth hostel, puts in the rooms according to his or her partner's instructions. When you have filled in a diagram, compare your drawing with the original.

❏   *Zum Beispiel:*   **A**   Also. Das Büro ist rechts im Erdgeschoß und die Küche ist auch im Erdgeschoß — links. Der Aufenthaltsraum ... usw.

**1 Beschreib diese Jugendherberge!**

**2 Beschreib diese Jugendherberge!**

**3 Beschreib diese Jugendherberge!**

**4 Beschreib diese Jugendherberge!**

# 7 THE YOUTH HOSTEL

▌ *Exercise 3   Where are the dormitories?*

In this activity you take it in turns to ask your partner where the rooms are in the youth hostel. Each of you knows where some rooms are and before doing the exercise you must copy your diagram into your exercise book. Then add other rooms to it by asking your partner where the rooms are which are listed on the right-hand side of the diagram. (Not all the spaces have symbols in them and when you finish you will have blank spaces.)

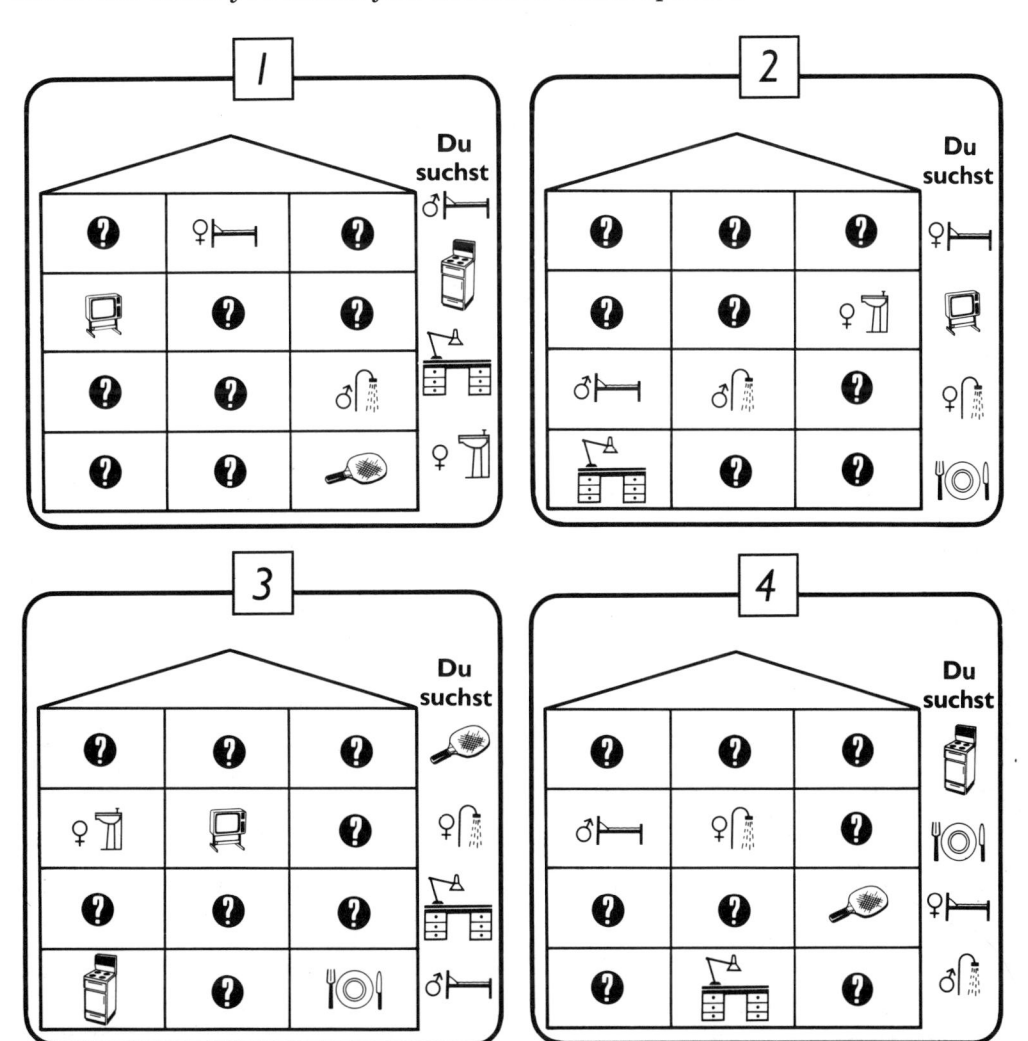

# 7 THE YOUTH HOSTEL ........................

❏ **Exercise 4  Making a simple booking**

In this activity you take it in turns to practise making bookings at youth hostels. First you have to find out if there is room and then you give details of the number of people and the length of stay. The partner who plays the part of the warden should note down the details of the booking.

❏ *Zum Beispiel:*  **A** Guten Tag (Guten Abend).
 **B** Guten Tag.
 **A** Haben Sie Platz, bitte? ❓ 🛏
 **B** Ja. Für wieviele Personen? 🛏✓  ❓ × 🧍
 **A** Drei Mädchen. 👩👩👩
 **B** Und für wieviele Nächte? (Wieviele Nächte wollen Sie/wollt ihr bleiben?)  ❓ × 🌙
 **A** Zwei Nächte. 2 × 🌙
 **B** In Ordnung. Ihre/Eure Ausweise, bitte.

Mach Reservierungen! Der Gast beginnt den Dialog und der Herbergsvater/die Herbergsmutter stellt folgende Fragen, usw.

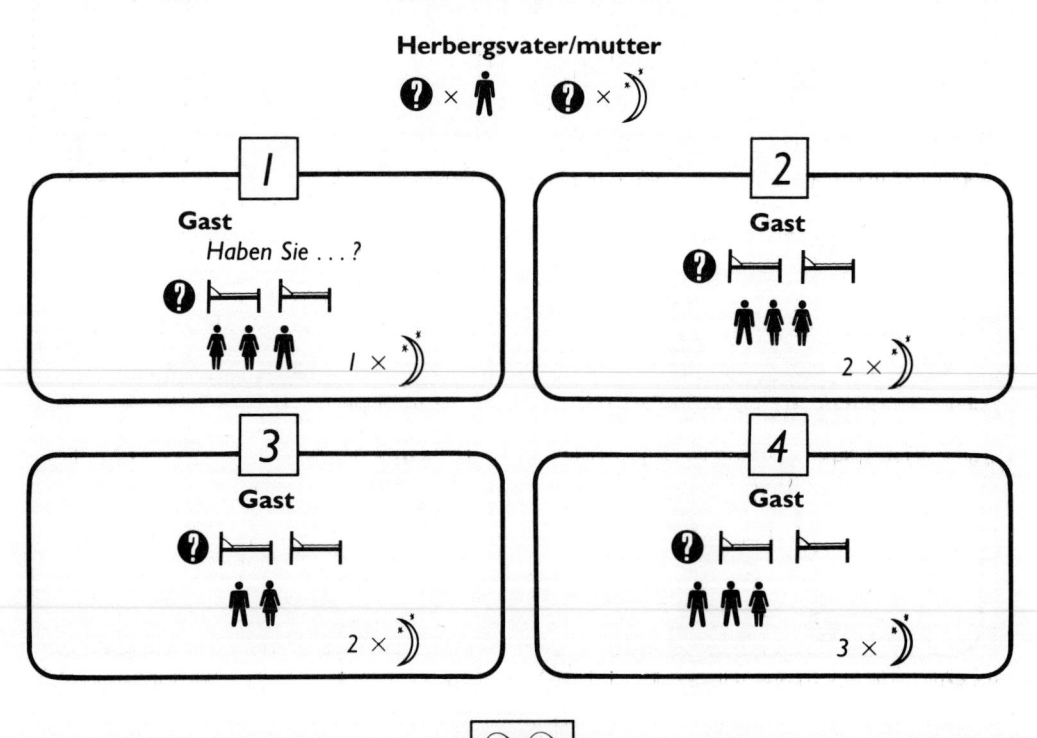

**Herbergsvater/mutter**
❓ × 🧍   ❓ × 🌙

**1**
Gast
Haben Sie ... ?
❓ 🛏 🛏
👩👩🧍   1 × 🌙

**2**
Gast
❓ 🛏 🛏
👩👩👩   2 × 🌙

**3**
Gast
❓ 🛏 🛏
👩👩   2 × 🌙

**4**
Gast
❓ 🛏 🛏
🧍👩🧍   3 × 🌙

36

# 7 THE YOUTH HOSTEL

### Exercise 5  Making a more complicated booking

In this activity you take it in turns to make a booking and in addition you ask for sheets and then ask where the dormitories are. The person playing the part of the warden should make a note of the details of the booking.

*Zum Beispiel:* (as for Exercise 4 plus:)
- **A** Brauchen Sie/Braucht ihr Bettwäsche?
- **B** Ja. Zweimal, bitte.
- **A** Das kostet 2.00 DM pro Person.
- **B** Danke. Wo sind die Schlafräume?
- **A** Die Jungenschlafzimmer sind im ersten Stock und die Mädchen schlafen im zweiten Stock.

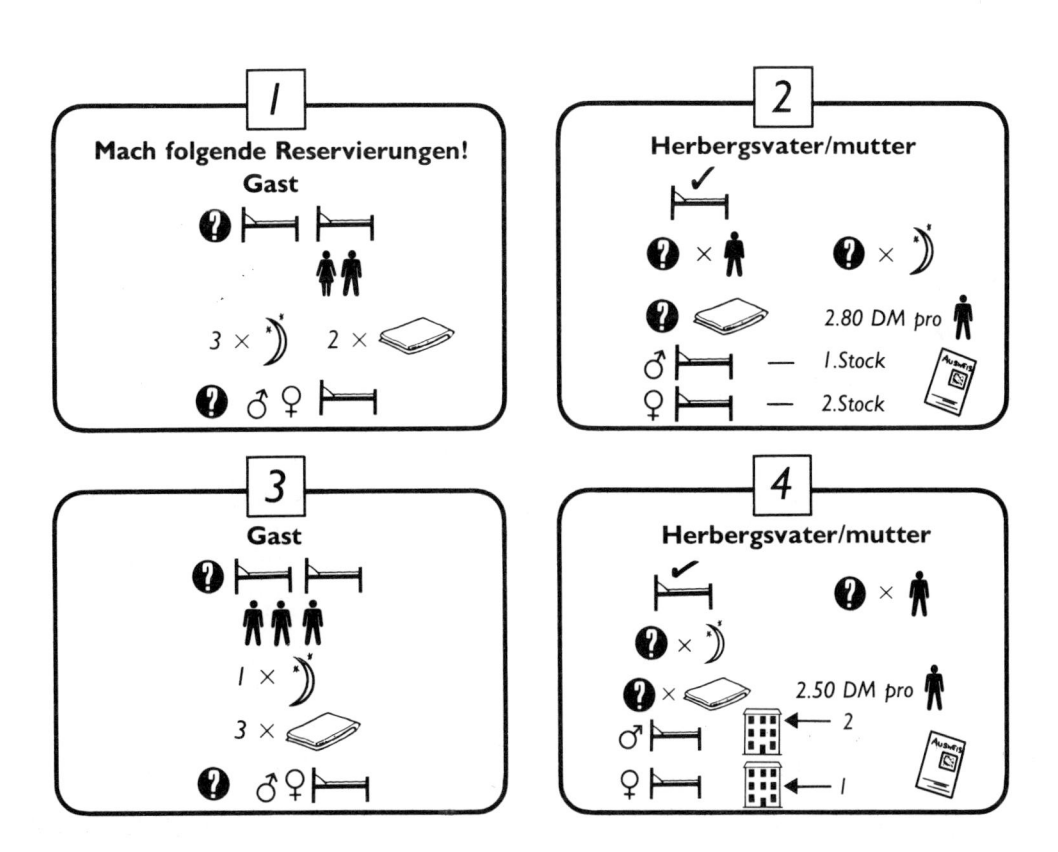

# 8 CAMPING ...........................

**Exercise 1   What do you say when you book in?**

The phrases given below are required in later exercises when you practise booking into a campsite. Study the symbols and the phrases and then find a partner and test each other.

Things that the person at reception and the camper may need to say:

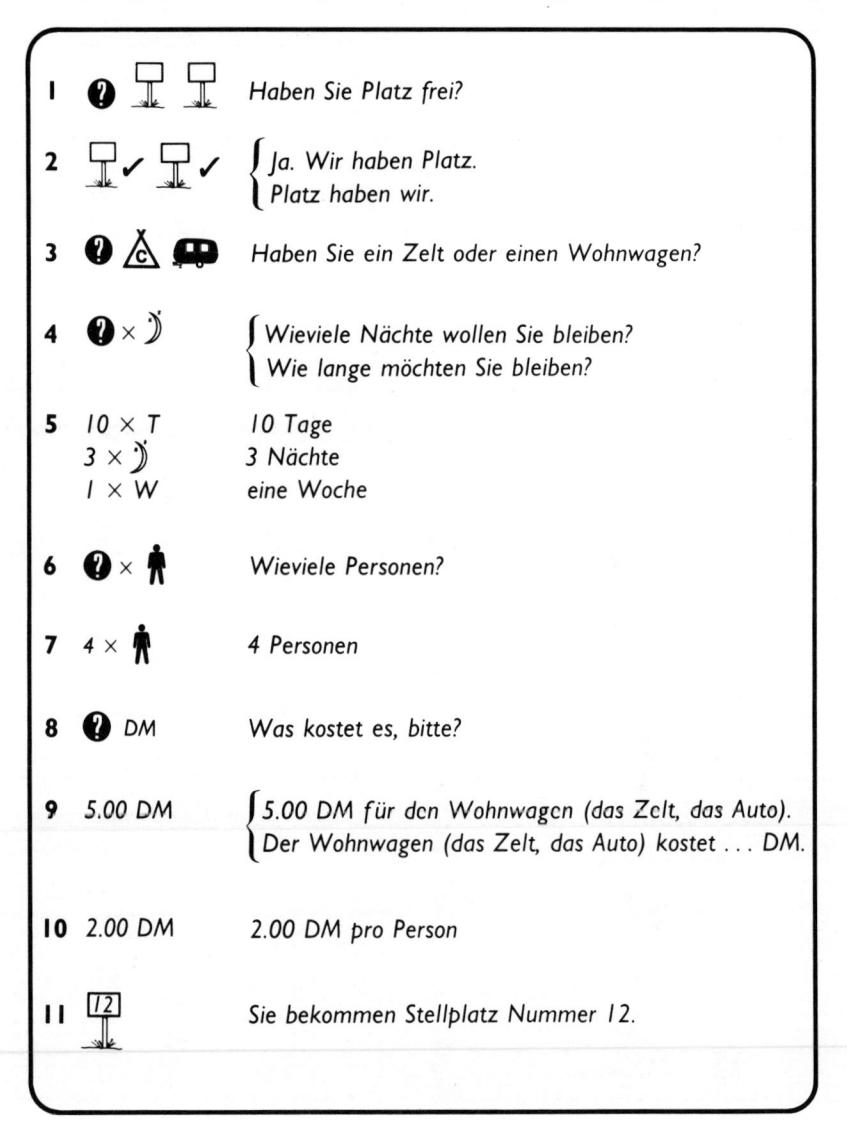

| | | |
|---|---|---|
| 1 | ❓ 🪧 🪧 | Haben Sie Platz frei? |
| 2 | 🪧✓ 🪧✓ | { Ja. Wir haben Platz. <br> Platz haben wir. |
| 3 | ❓ ⛺ 🚐 | Haben Sie ein Zelt oder einen Wohnwagen? |
| 4 | ❓ × 🌙 | { Wieviele Nächte wollen Sie bleiben? <br> Wie lange möchten Sie bleiben? |
| 5 | 10 × T <br> 3 × 🌙 <br> 1 × W | 10 Tage <br> 3 Nächte <br> eine Woche |
| 6 | ❓ × 🧍 | Wieviele Personen? |
| 7 | 4 × 🧍 | 4 Personen |
| 8 | ❓ DM | Was kostet es, bitte? |
| 9 | 5.00 DM | { 5.00 DM für den Wohnwagen (das Zelt, das Auto). <br> Der Wohnwagen (das Zelt, das Auto) kostet ... DM. |
| 10 | 2.00 DM | 2.00 DM pro Person |
| 11 | 🪧12 | Sie bekommen Stellplatz Nummer 12. |

# 8 CAMPING

❏ **Exercise 2  Booking in**

Now you can practise booking into a campsite. The camper should note down the details of the cost and of the plot number and the proprietor should note details of the number of people, whether they have a tent or a caravan and how long they want to stay for. After each exercise check to see that the communication was successful.

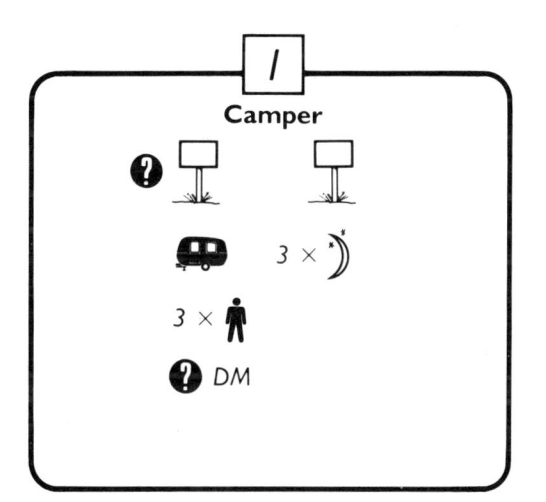

**1  Camper**

? 3 × 🌙
3 × 👤
? DM

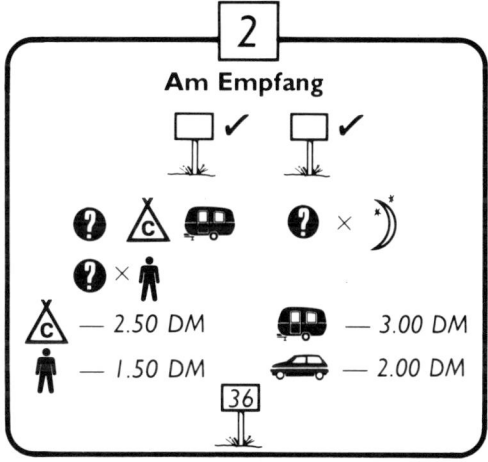

**2  Am Empfang**

✓ ✓
? 🏕 🚐   ? × 🌙
? × 👤
🏕 — 2.50 DM    🚐 — 3.00 DM
👤 — 1.50 DM    🚗 — 2.00 DM
36

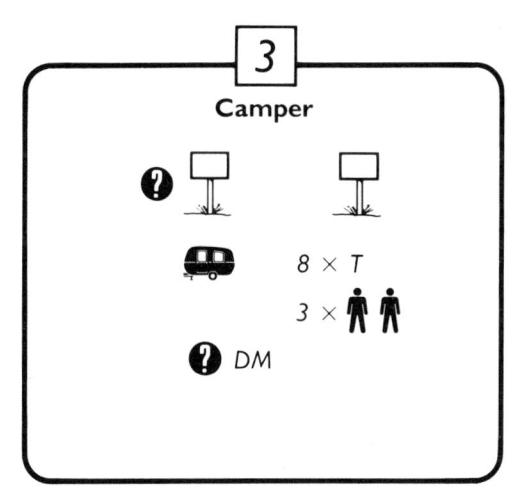

**3  Camper**

?
8 × T
3 × 👤👤
? DM

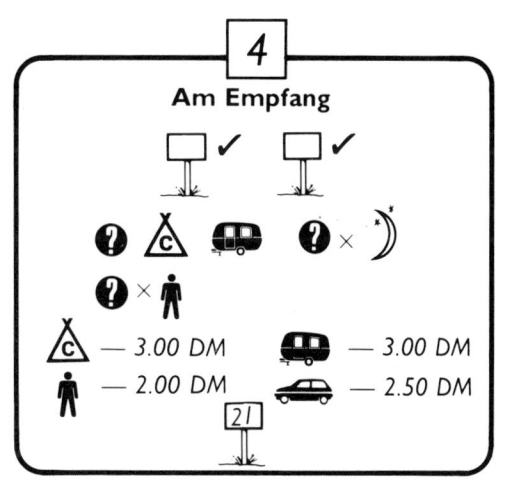

**4  Am Empfang**

✓ ✓
? 🏕 🚐   ? × 🌙
? × 👤
🏕 — 3.00 DM    🚐 — 3.00 DM
👤 — 2.00 DM    🚗 — 2.50 DM
21

# 8 CAMPING

### Exercise 3  Campsite amenities

Learn the vocabulary given below for the amenities on a campsite and then test each other before doing the exercises which come next.

| | | |
|---|---|---|
| 1 | | der Aufenthaltsraum |
| 2 | | das Telefon |
| 3 | | das Lebensmittelgeschäft |
| 4 | | das Restaurant |
| 5 | | das Schwimmbad |
| 6 | | die Duschen |
| 7 | | das Büro |
| 8 | | der Fernsehraum |
| 9 | | die Bar |
| 10 | | der Parkplatz |
| 11 | | Tischtennis |
| 12 | | das Café |
| 13 | | der See |

# 8 CAMPING

### Exercise 4  At the campsite

In this activity you exchange information with your partner to find out about all the facilities available at various campsites. Make a note of the facilities and then later write about what the various sites have to offer as follows:

   Am ersten Campingplatz gibt es ein Restaurant, einen Fernsehraum, einen Parkplatz, usw.

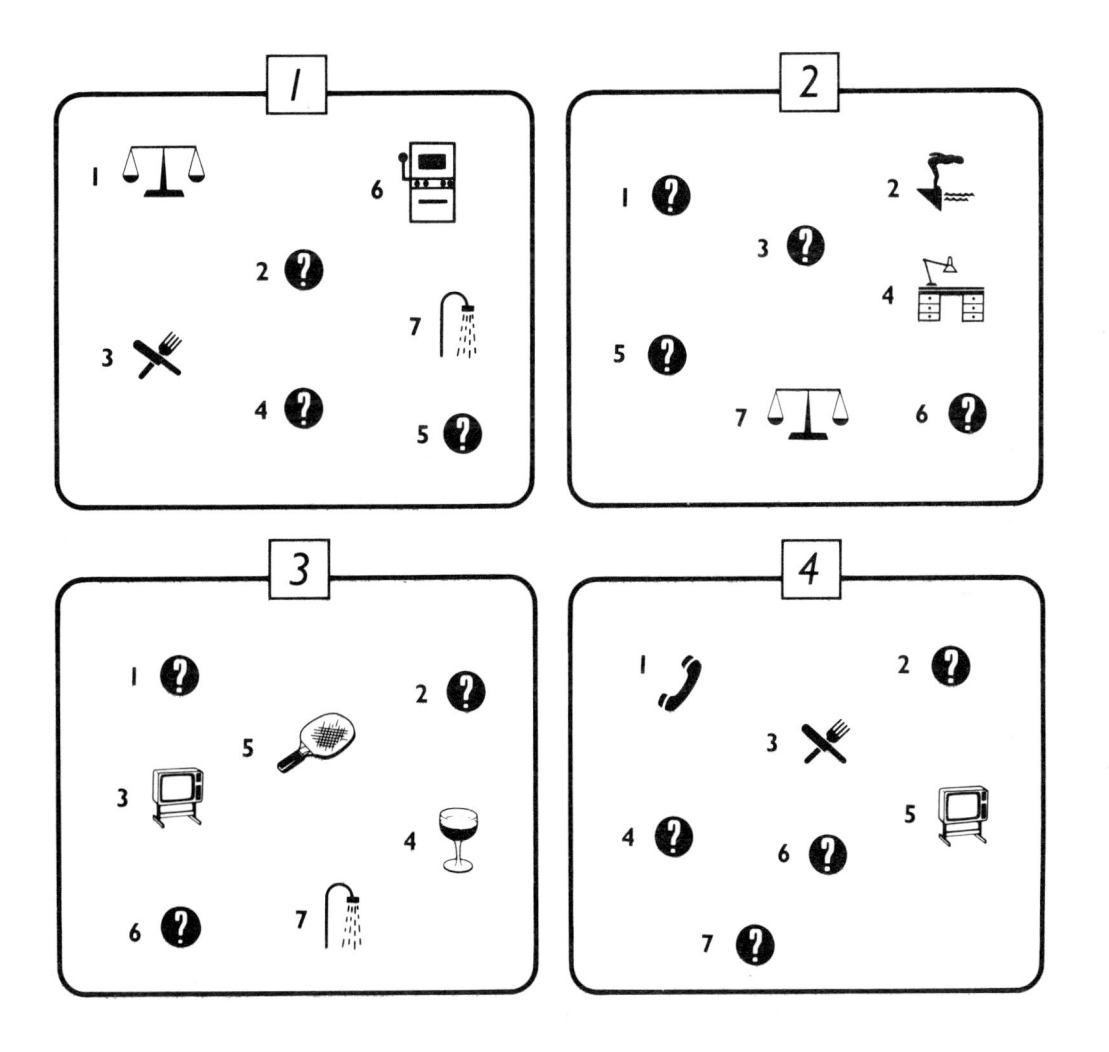

# 8 CAMPING

**Exercise 5   Checking the details**

In this activity one person has information about a campsite which is out of date or inaccurate and he or she checks the details with the other person, who has the up-to-date information. Make notes of the correct details and then later write it up as follows:

Campingplatz Bühlfeld.
Dieser Campingplatz hat ein Schwimmbad, ein Lebensmittelgeschäft und ein Restaurant. Es kostet 2.50 DM pro Person pro Nacht. Der Stellplatz kostet 3.00 DM und das Auto 2.00 DM.

*Zum Beispiel:*   **A**   *Am Campingplatz Bühlfeld gibt es ein Schwimmbad?*
                  **B**   *Ja.*
                  **A**   *Und einen Fernsehraum?*
                  **B**   *Nein. Es gibt keinen Fernsehraum. (Er hat keinen.)*
                  **A**   *Es kostet 2.50 DM pro Person pro Nacht?*
                  **B**   *Nein. Jetzt kostet es 3.00 DM.*
                  *usw.*

### 1
**Die Wahrheit**
*Campingplatz Hochwald*

2.50 DM pro Person pro Nacht
2.00 DM Stellplatz
1.50 DM Auto

### 2
**Ist das alles wahr?**
*Campingplatz am See*

2.00 DM × 👤 × 🌙
1.60 DM
1.80 DM 🚗

### 3
**Die Wahrheit**
*Campingplatz Berghof*

2.10 DM × 👤 × 🌙
2.00 DM
1.50 DM 🚗

### 4
**Ist das alles wahr?**
*Campingplatz Seeblick*

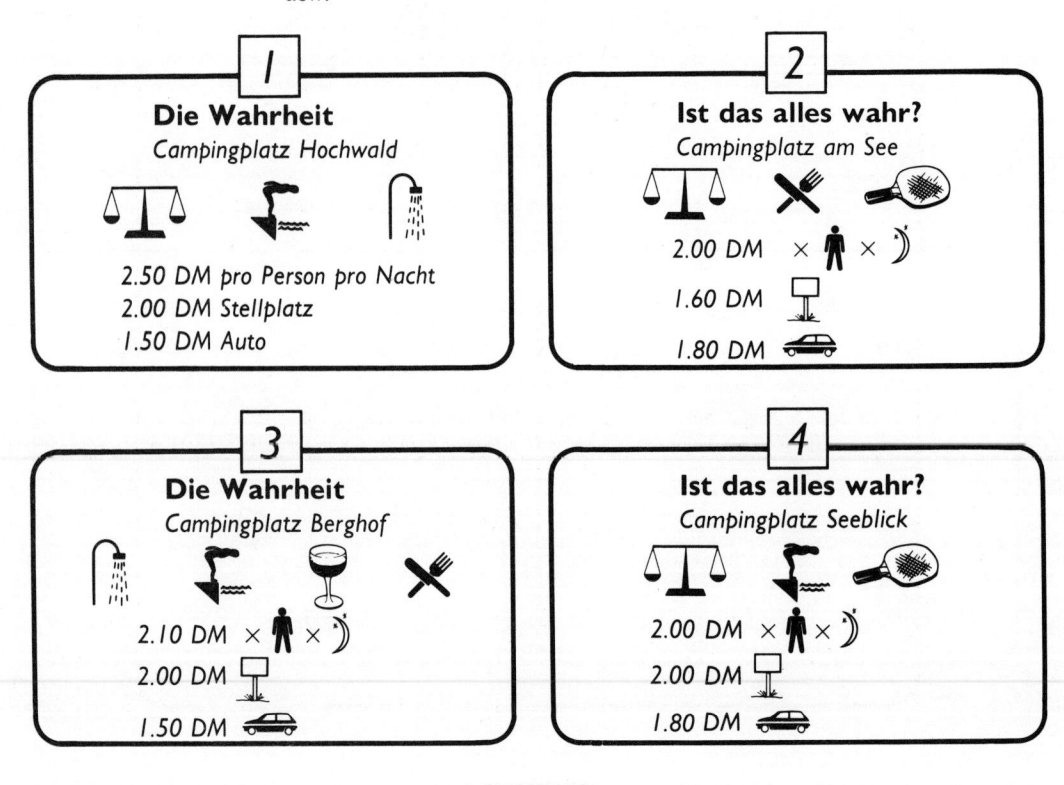

2.00 DM × 👤 × 🌙
2.00 DM
1.80 DM 🚗

# 9 HOLIDAY ACTIVITIES

### Exercise 1   Holiday activities

In this exercise you practise the German for the activities you can do on holiday. Study the text and the symbols and then test each other when you are ready.

| 1 | man kann segeln |
| 2 | man kann surfen |
| 3 | man kann reiten gehen |
| 4 | man kann angeln |
| 5 | man kann das Schloß besichtigen |
| 6 | man kann das Museum besichtigen |
| 7 | man kann Tennis spielen |
| 8 | man kann zum Schwimmbad gehen / man kann schwimmen gehen |
| 9 | man kann zum Strand gehen |
| 10 | man kann in die Disko gehen |
| 11 | man kann Fahrräder mieten |
| 12 | man kann einen Ausflug machen |
| 13 | man kann wandern gehen / man kann Wanderungen machen |

# 9 HOLIDAY ACTIVITIES ......................

**Exercise 2** *What can you do and what does it cost?*

In this activity you and your partner take it in turns to find out what you can do at certain holiday centres and then what some of the activities cost. The person asking the questions makes a note of all the information obtained and checks back later to see whether the communication was successful.

Zum Beispiel:
- **A** Was kann man am Freizeitzentrum Waldweg machen?
- **B** Man kann reiten gehen, angeln und Fahrräder mieten.
- **A** Was kostet es reiten zu gehen?
- **B** 11.00 DM pro Stunde.
- **A** Und wieviel kostet es ein Fahrrad zu mieten?
- **B** 8.00 DM pro Stunde.

### Stell Fragen über folgende Freizeitzentren!

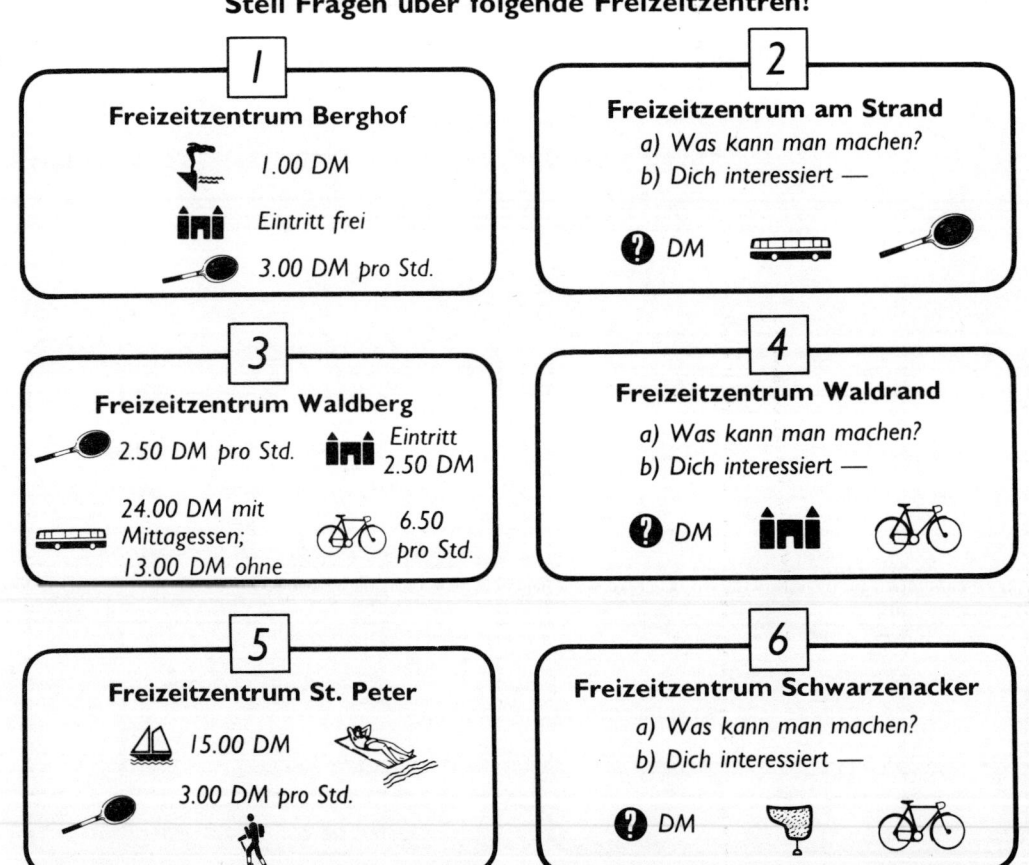

**1 Freizeitzentrum Berghof**
- 1.00 DM
- Eintritt frei
- 3.00 DM pro Std.

**2 Freizeitzentrum am Strand**
- a) Was kann man machen?
- b) Dich interessiert —
- ? DM

**3 Freizeitzentrum Waldberg**
- 2.50 DM pro Std.
- Eintritt 2.50 DM
- 24.00 DM mit Mittagessen; 13.00 DM ohne
- 6.50 pro Std.

**4 Freizeitzentrum Waldrand**
- a) Was kann man machen?
- b) Dich interessiert —
- ? DM

**5 Freizeitzentrum St. Peter**
- 15.00 DM
- 3.00 DM pro Std.

**6 Freizeitzentrum Schwarzenacker**
- a) Was kann man machen?
- b) Dich interessiert —
- ? DM

# 9 HOLIDAY ACTIVITIES

### Exercise 3   Which holiday centre suits them? A puzzle

Imagine that you and your partner are helping to suggest where people could go on holiday. You first find out what sort of thing they like to do and then, when you have got information about what is available at various holiday centres, you recommend a suitable centre. Do the exercise in three stages:
  1) Find out with your partner what people like doing. Note it down.
  2) Find out with your partner what you can do at the holiday centres. Note it down.
  3) Work out the best choice for each person. Write it down.

*Zum Beispiel:*   **1)**  **A**  *Inge. Sie schwimmt gern. Was sonst noch?*
   **B**  *Sie fährt gern rad.*
   **A**  *Und Karl. Er geht gern reiten.*
   *usw.*
**2)**  **A**  *Was kann man am Freizeitzentrum am See machen?*
   **B**  *Mann kann reiten gehen und schwimmen gehen.*
   *usw.*
**3)**  **A**  *Also. Inge schwimmt gern und fährt gern rad. Sie könnte zum Freizeitzentrum im Grünen gehen, nicht wahr?*
   **B**  *Ja. Und Karl. Er geht gern reiten und . . .*
   *usw.*

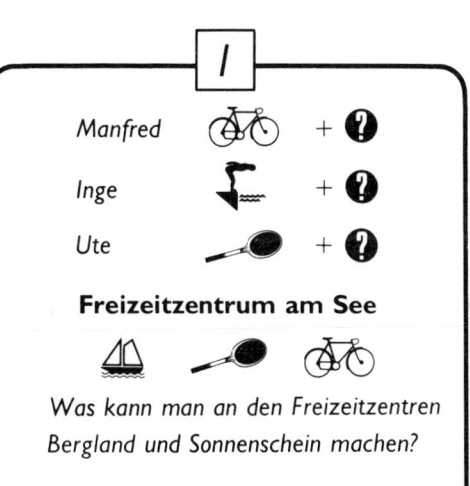

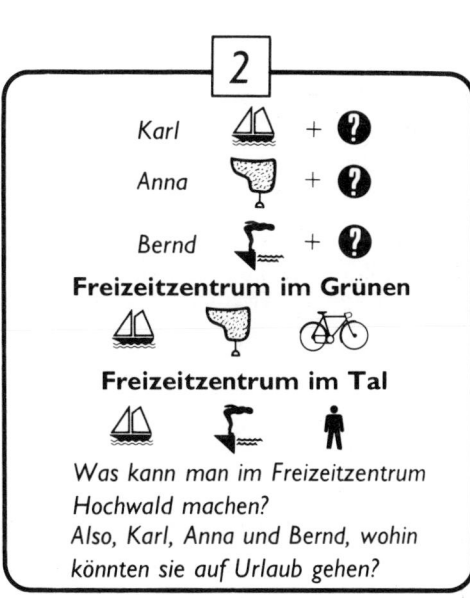

---

**1**

Manfred 🚲 + ❓
Inge 🏊 + ❓
Ute 🎾 + ❓

**Freizeitzentrum am See**
⛵ 🎾 🚲

Was kann man an den Freizeitzentren Bergland und Sonnenschein machen?

Also, Ute, Inge und Manfred, wohin könnten sie auf Urlaub gehen?

---

**2**

Karl ⛵ + ❓
Anna 🍷 + ❓
Bernd 🏊 + ❓

**Freizeitzentrum im Grünen**
⛵ 🍷 🚲

**Freizeitzentrum im Tal**
⛵ 🏊 🚶

Was kann man im Freizeitzentrum Hochwald machen?
Also, Karl, Anna und Bernd, wohin könnten sie auf Urlaub gehen?

# 10 HOLIDAY PLANS ..........................

**Exercise 1  Where are they going and when?**

In this activity you find out from each other where people are going on their holiday and between what dates. Make notes and write the information up later as follows:

Tania fährt vom 10. August bis zum 21. August nach Schweden.

Zum Beispiel:  A  *Wohin fährt Sven?*
B  *Er fährt in die Schweiz. Wann fährt er?*
A  *Vom 13. Juli bis zum 23. Juli.*
usw.

**Note:** vom 13. Juli = vom dreizehnten Juli

If you need to revise the countries, see Section 4, Exercise 4, page 23. One new country has been included — Amerika.

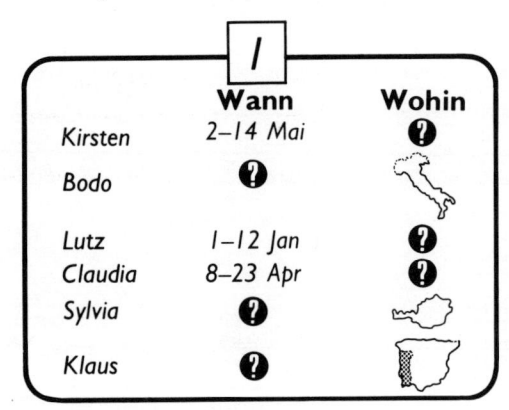

### 1

| | Wann | Wohin |
|---|---|---|
| Kirsten | 2–14 Mai | ? |
| Bodo | ? | |
| Lutz | 1–12 Jan | ? |
| Claudia | 8–23 Apr | ? |
| Sylvia | ? | |
| Klaus | ? | |

### 2

| | Wann | Wohin |
|---|---|---|
| Karl | ? | |
| Monika | 18–30 Okt | ? |
| Manfred | 8–17 Aug | ? |
| Frank | ? | |
| Erika | 26 Dez–19 Jan | ? |
| Gabi | ? | |

### 3

| | Wann | Wohin |
|---|---|---|
| Eva | 1–18 Jan | ? |
| Erich | 24 Okt–14 Nov | ? |
| Ulrich | ? | |
| Bettina | ? | |
| Reinhardt | 30 Juli–14 Aug | ? |
| Barbara | ? | |

### 4

| | Wann | Wohin |
|---|---|---|
| Inge | ? | ? |
| Tobias | 12–29 Mär | ? |
| Heike | ? | |
| Heidrun | 1–15 Juni | |
| Mark | ? | |
| Bernd | 23 Apr–19 Mai | ? |

# 10 HOLIDAY PLANS

❏  *Exercise 2   Check the facts*

In this activity you check personal details of people and where they are going on holiday, when they are travelling and how they travel. Take notes of the information and write it up later as follows:

    Karl ist 18. Er wohnt in Hamburg und dieses Jahr fährt er vom 13. August bis zum 30. August nach Spanien. Er fliegt.

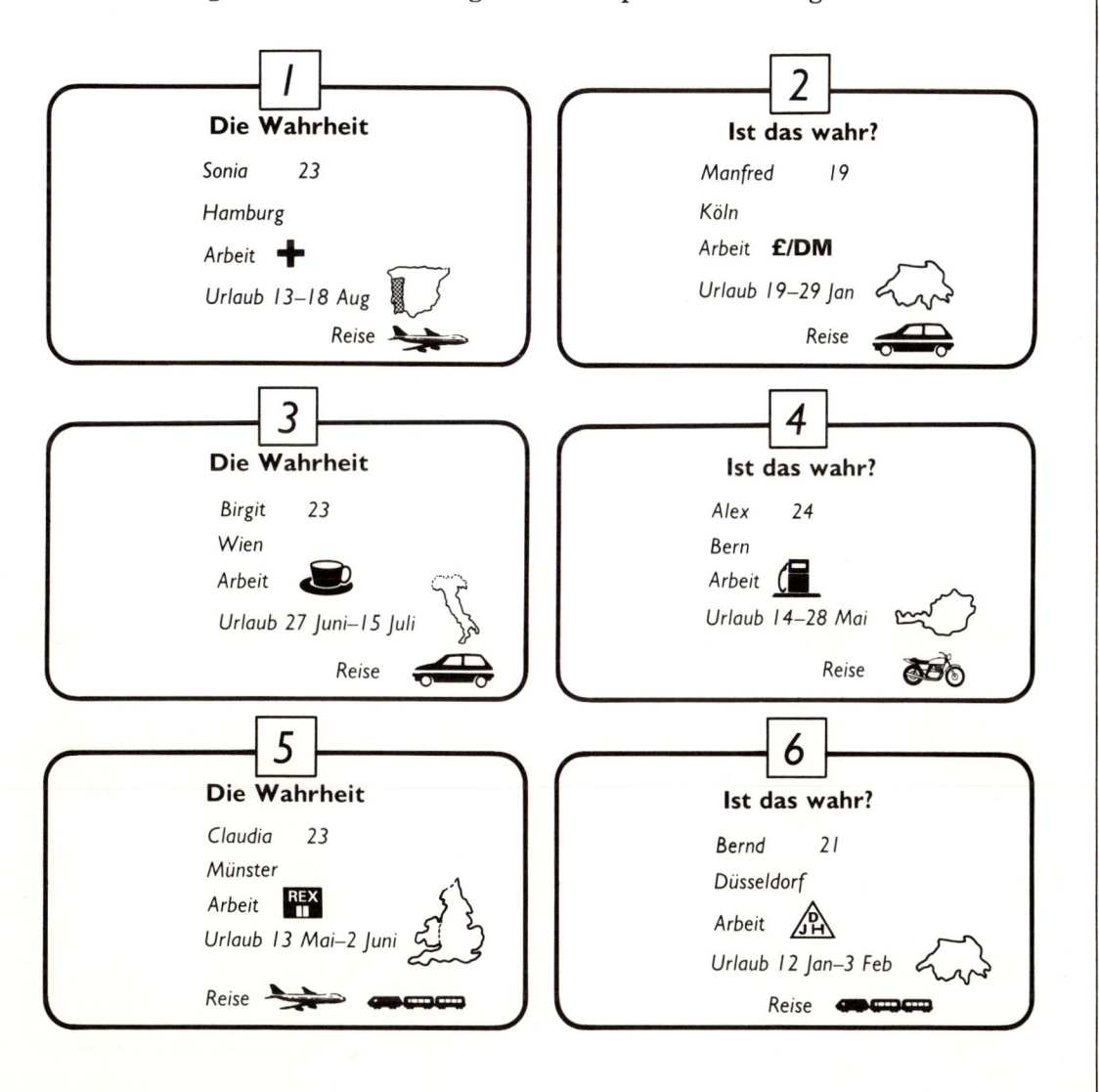

---

**1**

**Die Wahrheit**

Sonia   23

Hamburg

Arbeit   ✚

Urlaub 13–18 Aug

Reise

---

**2**

**Ist das wahr?**

Manfred   19

Köln

Arbeit   £/DM

Urlaub 19–29 Jan

Reise

---

**3**

**Die Wahrheit**

Birgit   23

Wien

Arbeit   ☕

Urlaub 27 Juni–15 Juli

Reise

---

**4**

**Ist das wahr?**

Alex   24

Bern

Arbeit   ⛽

Urlaub 14–28 Mai

Reise

---

**5**

**Die Wahrheit**

Claudia   23

Münster

Arbeit   REX

Urlaub 13 Mai–2 Juni

Reise

---

**6**

**Ist das wahr?**

Bernd   21

Düsseldorf

Arbeit   DJH

Urlaub 12 Jan–3 Feb

Reise

47

# 10 HOLIDAY ACTIVITIES ....................

**Exercise 3    Where are you going on holiday?**

In this exercise you find out about your partner's holiday plans. You have to find out the following:
- when he/she is going and returning
- where he/she is going
- how he/she is travelling
- who he/she is going with
- where he/she will be staying.

Make a note of the information and write it up later.

Zum Beispiel:
- A  Wohin fährst du dieses Jahr in Urlaub?
- B  Nach Deutschland.
- A  Wann fährst du?
- B  Am 13. Juli.
- A  Und wann kommst du zurück?
- B  Am 27.

- A  Wie fährst du?
- B  Wir fahren mit dem Zug.
- A  Mit wem fährst du?
- B  Mit meinem Freund.
- A  Wo wirst du wohnen?
- B  In Jugendherbergen und bei Freunden.

**Stell Fragen über Urlaubspläne!**

Urlaub — wohin?    Daten?
Reise — wie?    mit?
Unterkunft?

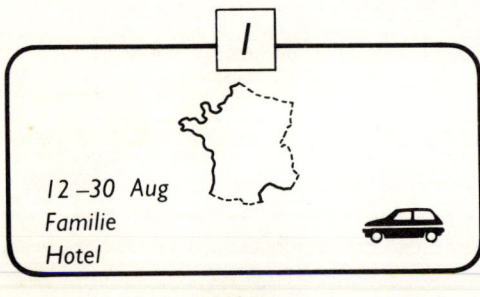

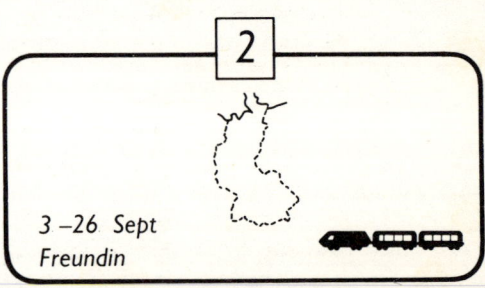

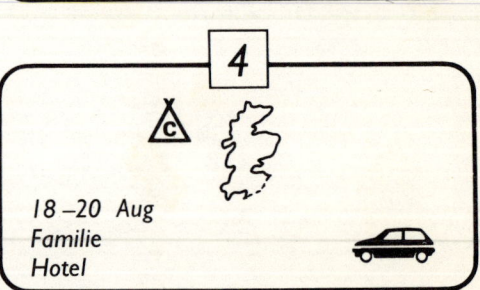

**1**
12–30 Aug
Familie
Hotel

**2**
3–26 Sept
Freundin

**3**
24 Jun–14 Jul
Freund

**4**
18–20 Aug
Familie
Hotel

48